WINGS AROUND SOUTH AMERICA

WINGS

AROUND SOUTH AMERICA

by

ALICE DALGLIESH

with pictures by

KATHERINE MILHOUS

NEW YORK

CHARLES SCRIBNER'S SONS

To

all those in

South America

who helped us,

with unfailing courtesy

and patience,

to know something

of their countries,

and to

Elisa Parada de Migel

whose letters of introduction

smoothed the way.

CONTENTS

Over the Caribbean to Colombia and the Canal
    On Our Way   3
    Pirates and Cartagena   11
    The Panama Canal   19

Over the Equator to Quito
    Over the Equator   27

Over the Desert to Peru
    Lima, City of the Kings   47
    At the Foot of El Misti   62

Over the Sea and Desert to Chile
    Santiago de Chile   75

Over the Mountains to Argentina
    The Great Mountains   87
    The City of Good Airs   93

Over the Rivers and Forests to Brazil
    The Busy City of São Paulo   103
    Down to Rio   113

Up the Coast of Brazil
    Bahia, City of Churches   129
    Adventure on the Coast   139

The Homeward Way
    Islands on Guard   147

OVER THE CARIBBEAN TO COLOMBIA AND THE CANAL

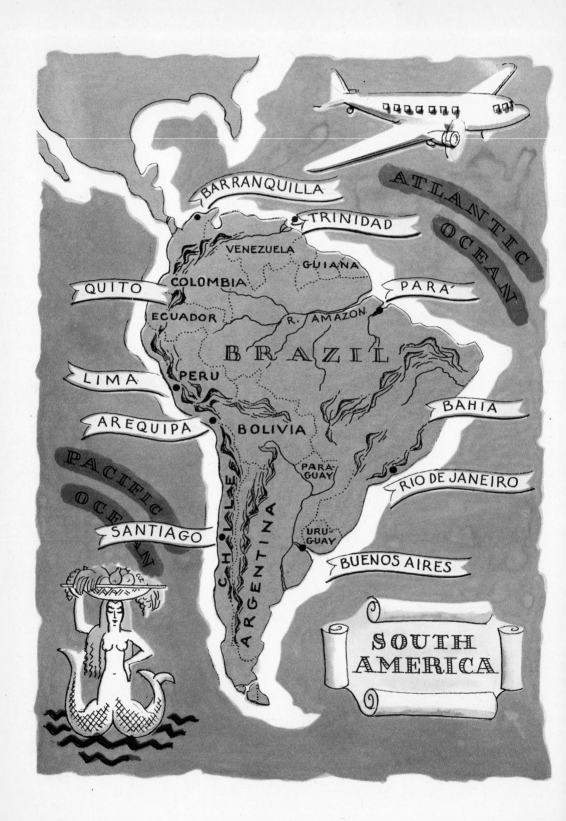

ON OUR WAY

P ANAGRA! PANAGRA!" Two Indian children watching
their sheep on a mountain slope in Ecuador look up
into the sky. The little girl shifts her baby brother to
a more comfortable position on her back. "Panagra!"

It sounds like an Indian word but it is really the trade name
of Pan American Grace Airways. As the long silver planes fly
overhead, the Indians say "Panagra!" using the word as if it
meant "airplane." They stop what they are doing to watch
the plane out of sight.

Before the airplane came to South America it was difficult
to travel from town to town or from one country to another.
On the west coast the Andes form a great mountain wall, there
are deserts where rain seldom, if ever, falls, and there are few
railroads. On the east coast there are jungles and wide rivers
with swift, muddy waters. Once it took days or weeks, even
months, to travel from one town to another. Now it takes only
a day or a few hours.

At first the Indians were alarmed and puzzled when the
great silver birds flew overhead, or roared down to rest at their

3

airports. Here was something as strange as the Spanish con-querors who came hundreds of years ago in their shining armor. What was this flying creature? Some called it the Thunder Bird. Others called it the Flying Llama. Soon the Indians became accustomed to airplanes and ceased to wonder, though not to be curious, about them.

The airplane has changed the whole life of South America, especially on the west coast. Children who live beyond the Andes, in the forest regions of Peru, can now fly down to boarding school in Lima. People who need to go to hospitals for operations use the planes to take them quickly to big cities. Business men travel by plane. Even flowers travel. Huge bunches of the flowers that grow in the cool air of the moun-tains, carnations and snapdragons and arum lilies, are flown to Panama, where only tropical flowers grow. Boxes of beautiful, fragile orchids travel by plane from Ecuador to North America, or south to Argentina.

Best of all, those of us from North America who want to meet our neighbors to the south can now fly from country to country in a shorter time than it would take to go by boat. We can have time to see something of the cities and villages and the people who live in them. We can see towns that are far inland or up in the mountains, not only those on the coast.

Two of us, going to South America to collect material for writing and illustrating a history book, are going to fly almost all the way around the continent. You may join us if you will. Neither of us has flown before. We have no idea how we shall like air travel, but we shall have every opportunity to find out, for we are going to fly in all kinds of planes, in seaplanes, large and small, in swift land planes, and in the largest and swiftest of all—the stratoliners. For the artist, South America is entirely new, for me it is not altogether so because, although I am an American, I was born in Trinidad, which is only about twenty miles off the coast of South America.

No, we do not think that two months will give us time to find out "all about South America." But it will be time enough to get quick impressions of the country, impressions to be sketched and written down while they are still "hot." We shall see all kinds of places and all kinds of people. In our travels we shall meet people who are much like those of the United States in some ways and different in others. We shall see the greatest contrast between the old and the new, for South America is a continent of contrasts. We shall see Indians, Negroes, people of pure Spanish or Portuguese descent, policemen, milkmen, streetcleaners, soldiers, priests, all those who help to make up the life of a country.

Now we are ready to start. We have had smallpox vaccination and typhoid inoculations. We have our passports, our fingerprints, our certificates of good conduct from the police, our identification photographs for countries that require them, for this is war time and countries are careful about the people they admit.

Packing our suitcases is a problem. We can take seventy-seven pounds of luggage each, and we need warm clothes for places high up in the mountains as well as many cool clothes for places that are in the tropics. The artist has to allow a good deal of weight for her sketch books and painting materials. We carry our coats and our cameras, but whenever we go on

a plane we must give up our cameras and have them returned
to us after we reach our destination. It is an army regulation
that no one is allowed, without a permit, to take photographs
from a plane.

Our big "clipper" leaves from Miami. Very early in the
morning we drive to the International Airport with its handsome buildings. There we have our tickets checked, our baggage weighed, and are weighed ourselves.

A bell rings and a voice calls through a megaphone: "Plane
for Barranquilla!" That is *our* plane. Our adventure has
begun! We go through a doorway which looks like the entrance to a train platform, and down to the dock where the
seaplane *Colombian* is riding on the water. She is silver, with
red stripes on her wings.

We go on board. Inside the plane are six cabins, or compartments, each accommodating four people. There are a
kitchen and a dressing room. Through an open door we can
see the cockpit, where the pilot, co-pilot, and radio operator sit.
This plane has round portholes like a ship, while land planes
have square windows.

The steward comes around. "Fasten your seat belts, please." The engines are tuning up. The plane begins to taxi over the water. Slowly it goes at first, then faster and faster and faster, the spray splashing against the portholes. Suddenly, without even realizing the moment that we leave the water, we find that we are in the air and Miami is below us.

The first pale yellow streaks of dawn are in the sky. We climb gradually upwards. Now we are above the clouds. The sun is shining and the day is clear.

"Oh!" we say. "The clouds!" For there are many billowy, white ones that stand very high and seem to march past us like an army of snow men. They look very innocent, but these tall cumulus clouds are possible storm clouds. A pilot avoids them; he does not go through them more often than he can help. For the whitest, softest, fluffiest-looking cloud is not really "soft" at all when the plane goes through it. The combination of hot and cold air that has pushed the cloud up into a tall pillar gives the plane some nasty bumps.

On we go with scarcely any sensation of motion. We are delighted to find that we are not airsick and that we like the plane. On and on. This flight over the blue Caribbean Sea is

one of the most beautiful that an airplane can take. We look down through fleecy, white clouds to a sea of bright ultramarine. Where there are reefs or shallows there are lovely color effects in the clear water, all shades of blue, veridian green, even terra cotta. At one time, when there is a solid floor of white clouds beneath us, we see reflected on it the shadow of the plane. It is like a toy, quite small, and ringed around by a circular rainbow. One does not often see this strange effect, only when there is a good deal of moisture in the air and the sun is shining.

We fly over the island of Cuba with its red-roofed houses and its neat patchwork of sugar-cane fields. We land briefly to refuel, then we are off again for Jamaica. As we fly over the mountains, the air is rough and the plane plunges wildly. "Fasten seat belts!" Some of us feel a little airsick and we are glad when we glide down to the airport of Kingston. It is something to remember, this small white airport set against a background of blue-green mountains. Its roof is the brightest green, and it is fringed with scarlet poinsettias. We stay here long enough to refuel, to have a drink of lemonade, then we are off again.

Four hours without seeing land! The steward brings a table for each cabin and sets it with an attractive green cloth and white, unbreakable dishes. We have soup, a meat course and dessert; we wonder how so large a meal can be prepared in so small a kitchen. At this point I take out my fountain pen to write some notes, and we discover for ourselves the difficulties airplane companies must have with carrying liquids on a plane. For my pen has overflowed and the ink is everywhere, on the pen and in my purse! When the plane reaches a certain height the outside pressure on the pen diminishes, the inside pressure remains the same. This forces liquid out of the container. Airplane companies had to work out how liquids could best be handled on a plane. At first all kinds of things happened to liquids in vacuum bottles. Sometimes, when the cork was taken out the bottle exploded! Now liquids are kept in open containers or, when the plane reaches a height of 10,000 feet, the steward is careful to see that the vacuum containers are not tightly corked. In the large seaplanes liquids are actually heated on the plane, the land planes have no heating facilities. But there is nothing to do about a fountain pen. The best plan is to empty the ink before leaving and use a pencil on the plane.

The afternoon seems long to the more experienced travelling men and others who have made the trip before. They go peacefully to sleep. But *we* stay awake and watch the clouds and the ever-changing color of the sea. Part of the time we think about these thrilling countries to which we are going. We have been reading the history of the continent and, now we are nearing the countries themselves, the mass of detail vanishes and a few clear dramatic moments and personalities stand out. Peru! Its very name brings us romantic pictures of the Incas and their colorful civilization. Shall we really see the ruins of their cities; the places where once stood proud Temples of the Sun?

Two personalities stand out above all others: Simón Bolívar, the great Liberator who led five South American countries to freedom from Spain, José de San Martín, Liberator of Argentina and of Chile, and, with Bolívar, of Peru. Everywhere in

Spanish South America, we know we shall learn something of these two men. Already our guide books have shown us that their names are remembered in town and village and city. Plaza Bolívar, Plaza San Martín—over and over and over again. Once one has read of the Liberators they are never again vague names: always there is the picture of dark, tempestuous, dramatic Bolívar; handsome, selfless but equally dramatic San Martín.

Suddenly, "South America!" says some one, and every one is very wide awake. Below us, seemingly having appeared out of nothing, is the coast of Colombia, the republic named for Columbus. Only eight hours ago we were in another continent!

The plane circles, losing altitude for its landing, and we have our first view of a Latin American city. It is Barranquilla, chief port of Colombia, and it is laid out in the Spanish way that is to become so familiar to us. There is a central square or *plaza* and from this the streets radiate, crossing at right angles to make many neat squares. The plane banks as it turns, and suddenly all the red roofs seem to come up and hit us.

Down we come, so smoothly that we do not know the moment when our flying boat touches the water. Colored men

in white suits row out, attach a rope to the plane, and we are slowly towed into the dock. We keep our seats while the captain lands.

"All passengers ashore!" shouts the steward. And we step ashore in South America.

PIRATES AND CARTAGENA

OUR GREETING from the South American sun is a warm one, but in no time at all we are sitting under the trees in the cool green patio of our hotel. In the center of the patio is a beautiful blue swimming pool bordered with palm trees. Brown-skinned Colombian boys and girls splash in the water. Cool trade winds fan us. There are flowers everywhere and crotons, tall plants with variegated leaves that add color to tropical gardens. It is all very pleasant and rather unreal. We—sit—and—dream——

Plop! Something falls from the tree above us and lands at our feet. We are a little startled to see a large, rainbow-colored lizard looking at us.

"Don't mind *him*," says the man in charge of the swimming pool. "Just Charlie. He likes you should tickle him under the chin." But *we* do not like. Charlie stares at us solemnly, then goes on his way. Now we *know* we are in the tropics.

Barranquilla is a pleasant city. Many of the houses are bright-colored "villas," each with its name painted on it in huge letters. VILLA ELENA is a lively pink with magenta bougainvillea dripping over it. VILLA ROSA, which *should* be pink, is pale green, all set with palms and yellow hibiscus. VILLA LUIZA is vivid blue. At first we are a little dazed by the riot of color, the strange combinations that one sees in tropical South America. Soon we get used to it and fail to be startled even by a bright orange house with magenta bougain-villea and pink oleander. But the artist says, "This book will *have* to be printed in six colors, not four. No one could picture South America in four colors."

Although the gardens run riot as to color, they seem to suit their tropical setting. They are really lovely. Everywhere boys are busy with hoses, for this is the dry season, when for six months there is practically no rain.

There is, we notice, a strange odor in the air. As we go down towards the docks, we find it is the odor of coffee beans. Bananas and cocoa and coffee, ships take them constantly from Barranquilla. In the market, men are carrying huge bunches of bananas on their backs; donkeys are carrying everything imaginable. And the many interwoven smells are entirely past description.

We did not come here to see Barranquilla but to go to Cartagena, which will have a place in our history book. Cartagena is a very old city built by the Spanish in the sixteenth century. It is one of two fine old walled cities of the New World. The other city is San Juan in Porto Rico, which we shall see at the end of our journey.

There is no train to Cartagena; we must go by car. George, our colored chauffeur, comes from the West Indies, so he tells us. In fact he comes from Trinidad, my own native island. "The island too small for George," he says. "Colombia gives more opportunity."

At this moment our main interest is in the road. We have heard things about it.

"Is it a bad road, George?"

"No, lady, not a *bad* road."

But it *is* a bad road, one that can scarcely be called a road, with large parts under construction and detours, mostly through ploughed fields. It takes us four hours and a half to drive ninety miles, each way.

We start at five o'clock in the morning to avoid some of the heat. In the darkness the dim lights of the car show us that the road is full of strange shapes. As the sun rises, we see that the strange shapes are donkeys staggering along on their spindly legs under loads much too heavy for them. They are bound for the market at Barranquilla. Will they ever make it? Often men and boys ride on the already unbelievable load. As we drive farther out into the country, the road is dry and dusty. There is little water in the dry season and now most of the donkeys are carrying water jars, gourds, or barrels, one on each side.

The villages along the road are primitive and pretty in their own way. The small, thatched adobe houses are of such bright color that they put the villas of Barranquilla to shame. It is in one of these villages that we see Carlos, our first country boy.

Carlos is part Indian, part Negro, the mixture that in South

America is known as "Zambo." He is coming back from the river with water. The thin little burro carries two brightly painted gourds. Carlos rides high on the saddle, with crossed legs, not holding on to anything. He is ragged and quite different from the handsome Spanish boys in white suits that we have seen in the city. But Carlos looks happy, he grins at us. The village he lives in is something we would not believe if it were not before our eyes. There is a tiny plaza with a church of bright watermelon pink. On three sides of the square, and in the radiating streets, are rows of thatched adobe houses built right on the street. One is white with a wide green stripe around the lower half, and green doors. Another is orange with blue doors. Spanish houses have iron grille work over the windows, so these little houses have painted wooden grilles. They are Indian houses playing at being Spanish, like children dressed up in their mother's clothes. Most of them are neat and well painted. Through the open doors, however, we can see only a few sticks of furniture and we know that the people who live in these houses are very poor. Almost all through the country districts of South America the people work for large land-owners and are not well paid.

Carlos stops his donkey in front of the orange house and jumps off. We see, to our amusement, that the name painted over the door is *Hollywood*. A little girl comes through the doorway. She is wearing a faded cotton dress and carrying a plump, naked baby on her hip. Other small children of varying ages play in the road before the houses, their only clothing a covering of white dust that makes them look like gingerbread children dusted with flour. Our car goes on and we see no

more of Carlos and his village, but we have stayed long enough for the artist to put them on paper.

Through other painted villages, through banana plantations and sugar-cane fields. Now some of the villages are entirely Indian, with crude houses of mud and bamboo. The road gets worse. We bump along and swallow clouds of dust.

"George, did you say this wasn't a *bad* road?"

"Well, lady, it *do* seem to have got worse."

At this moment we drive bumpily over a dead alligator, and decide that dead alligator is worse than dead skunk. And before we have time to recover, we find the car almost in the ditch. A huge truck loaded with green bananas has swung round a corner on the wrong side of the road and crowded us off.

"Nearly got us," George grins. "They're *killers*, these Colombia drivers." We soon learn that taxi and truck drivers of this continent are the greatest hazards of travel. In Colombia we even see taxi drivers challenge each other with their cars, each refusing to give up the right of way.

More banana trucks! Worse road! But there in plain sight is Cartagena, its walls and forts making it look like a medieval city. As we drive into it, however, the city looks almost oriental; it is something out of the *Arabian Nights*. Houses are of every color and trimmed with elaborate iron balconies and grille work. Narrow streets teem with dark-skinned people dressed in white. Open-faced shops display the gayest of wares in their doorways. These are the first of the open shops that we shall see in the warm countries, shops that have no windows, whose whole fronts are shutters that roll up to display their goods.

Through the crowded streets, so narrow that driving is difficult, we go to the hotel. It is nearly ten o'clock and we would like a second breakfast. George speaks in Spanish to the man in charge; then angry Spanish words leap and fly around us. Hotter and hotter grows the argument. All kinds of thoughts go through our heads. Don't Colombians like us? Won't they even *feed* us?

"You can't stay here," says George, and we get back into the car. What has it all been about? Merely that the hotel insisted that nothing could be served before *eleven* and George thought that it should be served *now!* We are to learn that in this country hot arguments often mean little. For us, this argument means lunch at a small water- front restaurant which, after all, is nicer than the hotel. Boats poled by Negroes pass close to where we sit. The proprietor calls one to the sea wall, and then brings us a lobster

alive and angry and snapping its armored body. "Fine fresh
lobster?" Somehow it is a little too fresh for us, we prefer fish.

"We are going to see the Standard Oil plant," says George
as soon as we have had our lunch. We protest. Yes, we know
that Cartagena is an important oil port and has a pipeline laid
from the oil fields farther inland. But we refuse to see Standard
Oil; it is the *walls* we want. Cartagena was the city where
much of the gold that went to Spain from South America was
stored. It was often attacked by pirates and sometimes captured, which must have annoyed the Spaniards, who had put
some seventy million dollars into the building of the walls.

While we are still telling George what we want, we find
ourselves on the walls. We are actually driving along them,
and there is still space for two or more other cars. We get out
of the car and the blistering sun beats down on us. George says
it is 120° and we can believe it. In the bright sunlight the old
walls are a lovely soft cream
color. The green fronds of coconut palms wave above them.
Through the "windows" in the
walls, which are really gun
emplacements, and from which
cannon once pointed out to
sea, are glimpses of the water.
It is startlingly green. At in-
tervals along the walls are sentry boxes, from which Spanish
sentries once kept watch for
pirate ships.

We leave the walls and go up the steep, difficult road to La Popa, at the top of the hill. Here is the old convent, and the three rows of arches of the old monastery. Here, too, is the Virgin, who in the old days was trusted by the people to guard the city. Each year she is carried in procession down the steep hill to the grotto where she is said to have been found.

Once Cartagena was captured by the Welsh pirate, Henry Morgan, whose bold, bad deeds were known all along the Spanish Main. The story says that when the monks and nuns of La Popa saw the pirate ships coming into the harbor, they jumped from La Popa to the rocks below. They knew Morgan.

Now we are looking down at the red roofs of the city. Cartagena is a colored page from an old history book. How we wish we could turn back the pages! Then we would see the huge stones of the walls being put in place by half a million unfortunate sweating Negro slaves. We would see the big Spanish galleons at anchor in the harbor. And—we would see Henry Morgan himself.

It was the constant danger from pirates that made Colombia build some of its cities far from the coast. It would be pleasant to go to the beautiful capital city of Bogotá, high up in the mountains. There it is cool all the year round and in the heat of Cartagena we think longingly of it. But Bogotá means a special trip by airplane.

We wonder about the banana, coffee and cocoa plantations; about the emerald mines, and the jungles, where we cannot go. We would like to see orchids growing; there are hundreds of beautiful orchids in Colombia. But there are so many things to see—and so much of South America is still ahead.

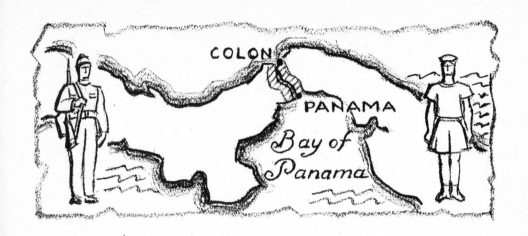

THE PANAMA CANAL

IT IS a short, easy trip from Barranquilla by land plane, a twenty-one-passenger Douglas DC3, to Panama, where we make connections for the plane that is to take us to Quito, capital of Ecuador.

Avianca, the local branch of Pan-American Airways, is evidently not as strict as some companies in its rules about animals travelling on planes, for a very long, very shiny dachshund is to travel with us. Solemnly she steps on the scales and is weighed, then her owners hurry her into a basket. On the plane we neither see nor hear her.

We fly over the sea, along the coast. It is not particularly interesting, until, beneath us, we see the Panama Canal. We have been losing altitude for the landing, and the temperature has been going higher as the plane goes lower. Just as we think we cannot stand any more heat, the steward closes every ventilator and takes out a large insecticide gun, with which he sprays the plane. He is very thorough about it, and the odor, mixed with the heat, is terrible. The passengers gasp for breath and complain. It is a Panama regulation, the steward explains. No mosquitoes may ride into Panama on planes!

When we land we are met by a doctor who, without a word, sticks a thermometer into each mouth. We wonder what will happen if one of us proves to have fever. Fortunately no one does.

When we drive from the airport to our hotel we can understand all these precautions, for the road goes through black, ugly swamps. We have heard the story of how malaria and yellow fever were conquered in the Canal Zone, but, with these swamps, there must still be mosquitoes. We notice that the houses not far from the swamps are screened. But at the hotel there are few screens and we can sit on the open verandah or walk in the garden without being bitten by a single mosquito. The reason is that when Colonel Gorgas and his staff worked to make the Canal safe from malaria and yellow fever, they made use of two important facts. *Anopheles*, the mosquito that carries malaria, likes to lay her eggs at the edges of brooks or running water, but she does not fly far from the place where she lives. *Stegomyia*, the mosquito that carries yellow fever, likes to lay eggs in swamps or standing water. Puddles or rain barrels near a house are favorite spots. It was not possible to clean up all the running water or swamps of the low-lying Canal Zone, but it *was* possible to put a film of kerosene over them, thus keeping the mosquito larvæ from breathing. If water around houses and in towns was cleaned up, *Anopheles* would not fly to them from water that was far away. Draining swamps wherever possible, clearing away brush, spreading kerosene and keeping a strict watch for standing water, did away with malaria and yellow fever in towns and cities. This was important for all low-lying tropical South America. Now the yellow flag of quarantine no longer flies over ships in South American ports. In the big cities you will not find screened houses or mosquito netting over beds. Each city, however, has to have a "mosquito patrol" constantly on guard, to watch for standing water and to fine householders who disobey regulations. In the jungle, mosquitoes still hold their own.

Our stay in Panama is short, but gives us time to see the Canal. Our hotel is in the Canal Zone, that strip of land ten miles wide and fifty miles long leased by the United States from the Republic of Panama. At the entrance to the Canal are twin towns named after Columbus, Cristóbal and Colón. Cristóbal is in the Canal Zone, Colón in Panama, but it is impossible to tell where one town begins and the other ends. They aren't pretty towns, for, especially in Cristóbal, there are too many gray boxlike houses with screens. Only the garden of the hotel holds a certain amount of enchantment, as looking over the low gray sea wall, through tall coconut palms, we see the ships entering the Canal. Most of them are freighters, carrying material for the building of new defenses.

Everything is very busy in the Canal Zone. The hotel clerk constantly answers the telephone. "No, we have no accommodations." "Yes, space for *one*, but you will have to share a room." The hotel is crowded with men in army and navy uniforms. Planes with army insignia on their wings roar overhead.

We spend one day taking a trip across the isthmus by train, so that we may really see the Canal. The train is full of soldiers in the Canal Zone uniform of olive-drab shorts and shirts, with green-lined sun helmets. Our guide book tells us that "Sun helmets are not much worn in Panama and are considered an affectation," but the army must not have read the guide book! Everywhere in the train are engineers who are working on the defenses. Groups of them sit together, studying maps and plans. It makes us feel the importance of the Canal.

From the train we have a good view of the Canal. We pass Gatún Lake. The bare, ghostly branches of trees show above the water, for this section was flooded when the water of the river was dammed to make a lake. We pass close to the locks that lift and lower the ships from the level of one lake to another. Everywhere there are tents, soldiers, army trucks, airplanes. Everywhere there are signs: CAMERAS FORBIDDEN. DEFENSE AREA. KEEP OUT.

We see something of the picturesque cities of Panama and Balboa, on the Pacific side of the Canal. From a little hill we get our first view of the Pacific Ocean. There on the waterfront is a statue of Vasco Núñez de Balboa himself, with sword upraised, claiming the Pacific Ocean for Spain. Again we have the strangest feeling of having stepped back into history.

Old Panama City, to which we drive, was once a fine city, but it is now nothing but ruins. This, once more, is Henry Morgan's work. Having heard that there was much gold in Panama City, he went to get it.

The people of Panama heard that the pirates were coming and so were ready. As Morgan and his men landed, the men of Panama City went out to meet them. Ahead of the towns-people, so the story says, went a herd of bulls, guided by six *vaqueros* or cowmen. These were supposed to gore the enemy. Unfortunately Morgan's men shot the *vaqueros* and the herd stampeded, trampling underfoot many of those whom they were supposed to protect. The city was set on fire by order of the governor, but there was still much of value left for the pirates.

The tower of the old Cathedral still stands, so do other walls

here and there. Trees have spread curious, grasping roots over the ruins as if to swallow them up. Pigeons coo in the ruins of the Cathedral; pelicans fly lazily overhead. There is a strong feeling of the past—it might be only yesterday that Henry Morgan was here. The place is so untouched, so evidently not "fixed up" for tourists. There is a small restaurant, but in our country there would probably be half a dozen hot-dog stands and along the road placards would anounce: *Don't miss Henry Morgan's Ruins. Lunch at the Pirate Inn.* Oh, South America, keep your historical spots unspoiled!

Going back to "new" Panama City, we see the golden altar that was in one of the churches of old Panama. The story says that the monks, hearing that Henry Morgan was on his way, whitewashed the altar so that the pirate never knew it was made of gold. We don't believe the story; Henry Morgan was too smart to be taken in so easily! It seems more likely, as we read elsewhere, that the altar was of wood and was given its gold coating *after* it was moved to new Panama City.

Old Panama City is desolate indeed, but the new city is very much alive. The streets are lined with the most cosmopolitan shops, like oriental bazaars, Indian, East Indian, Japanese, Chinese, where all kinds of goods and curios are sold. We look at them hastily, but leave the shopping to the regular tourist who finds them a paradise indeed.

OVER THE EQUATOR TO QUITO

OVER THE EQUATOR

Now comes one of the most thrilling of our flights. For the first time we are to fly over the Andes, "las Cordilleras" as the South Americans call the tremendous ranges that run north and south. For years the high, wild Cordilleras shut Quito and the mountain villages of Ecuador off from the world. Then with great difficulty and at the cost of many lives, a railroad was constructed and a train made the trip in two days. There followed the "Quito Express," making the trip in one day. Since 1939 passenger planes fly from Guayaquil on the coast to Quito in one hour!

From Cristóbal to Buenos Aires, our air line is to be Panagra. We fly first over the Canal; we can see the locks, and the ships going through them, quite clearly from the air. Then we fly over the sea and finally turn inland.

Look down! These mountains beneath us are different from any we have seen. Fold after fold of crumpled yellow-green velvet, with patches of darker green dotted with white flowering trees and small Indian villages. Here and there a curl of smoke rises from a solitary hut. Clouds race against the taller peaks, sometimes hiding them entirely.

We stay overnight at the very European-looking town of Cali in Colombia. Here we would feel many miles from home if there were not large signs advertising one of the most popular of our own "movies." At dinner the hotel proprietor gives every one in the dining room a beautiful white or purple orchid. The next day, with orchids pinned to our coats, we are on the way to Quito.

If the mountains seemed strange yesterday, today they are even more mysterious. As we go higher there is almost no vegetation. The mountain tops are bare, brown volcanic rock with different colorings where there are mineral deposits. As we look down on them they are for all the world like huge prehistoric animals asleep, their gray-brown skin lying in wrinkled folds.

"If we had to land, what would happen?" we ask the purser.

"Oh, there are several emergency landing fields," he says reassuringly. "If one motor failed we could still make a landing field." Then he tells us, "In a few minutes we shall cross the equator."

We have heard of the ceremony of crossing the equator on ships, when Neptune and his court come aboard. What happens on a plane, we wonder. In a short time we find out. Flying at an altitude of almost fourteen thousand feet, between tall mountain peaks, the plane makes a couple of sudden dips —its salute to the equator.

But that is not all. Panagra gives us our equator certificates, ridiculously pompous parchments stating that Jupiter Rex,

King of the Sky, has graciously permitted us to fly over the equator. Henceforth we are to be known by the name of that great vulture of the Andes; we are Condors!

The plane is coming down. The buildings of the Quito airport are set against a tall mountain, and they are yellow with red roofs. Around them are gardens with snapdragons, marigolds, carnations, and shasta daisies that reach to our shoulders.

We walk slowly when we land, for suddenly we are beginning to feel very strange indeed. In the plane we did not feel the altitude because we were sitting still, but as we walk we begin to feel the effects of the altitude of over nine thousand feet. To walk is an effort. We breathe deeply, but feel as if nothing at all is going into our lungs. The air is thin and there is little oxygen in it. Some do not mind it; others have *soroche* or mountain sickness. There is nothing much more unpleasant than *soroche*, for it is seasickness plus headache, plus shortness of breath, plus a feeling that one's legs are about to fold up. Even when we feel better we have to walk slowly and go up stairs very slowly, or our hearts beat much too fast for comfort. The Indians of this region are built for mountain living; they are short and squat, with large chests to accommodate large lungs.

It is Sunday morning and, as we drive from the airport, the road is crowded with Indians. These are the Quito Indians, very light gold-colored people who look quite oriental. The men wear bright-colored *ponchos*. The women wear colored skirts over many petticoats, and bright shawls. Little girls are dressed like their mothers; boys like their fathers. Men, women, and children wear men's felt hats with tall crowns.

The Indian houses are of white adobe, with red tiled roofs. Near them grow the stiff cactus plants which are almost as tall as the houses.

We are delighted with our introduction to Quito, but not so pleased to find that we can only get into one of the smaller hotels. However, its warm hospitality almost makes up for the stairs we have to climb, the lumpy beds, the ever-present smell of garlic. Cream-colored descendants of the Incas stand on the stairs waiting to answer bells. If we ring our bell, half-

a-dozen boys appear at once. They scurry silently away and return, unsmiling, with whatever it is that we want.

Until I get over my *soroche*, my wants are mostly tea and toast. At first our room is warm, for in the middle of the day the temperature is quite high. But as night comes, even though we are so near the equator, the most extraordinary chill comes with it. Nothing, we feel, will ever make us warm again. We crawl under the bed-covers, wearing all the warm garments we can find in our suitcases. Now we know why the Indians wear ponchos that, in the middle of the day, look warm and heavy. We could use a few ponchos ourselves.

QUITO PAGEANT

With *soroche* one does not sleep very well and, anyway, it would be difficult to sleep in Quito the first night.

Until after midnight there is the honking of automobile horns, for each car approaching a crossing is required to blow its horn. For an hour or two there is silence. Then, at about four o'clock, the streets are cleaned with energy and stiff brooms by pig-tailed Indians in short white trousers and red ponchos. The members of this particular tribe of Indians have the privilege of being street cleaners to the city, and they are proud of it. At five o'clock, the church bells begin. There are many, many bells in Quito and they are the loudest and harshest to be found anywhere.

> Bang! Bang! Bang!
> Get to church! Get to church!
> Get to church *at once!*
> Bang! Bang! Bang!

The bells of some cities plead gently. The Quito bells give orders and promise hell-fire to those who do not obey.

To see the life of the city one needs only to sit in the center square, the Plaza Independencia, and watch all that is going on around. It is one of the most colorful pageants to be seen in South America.

On one side of the Plaza is the government building where the President has his offices. On another is the big cream-colored cathedral where General Sucre, follower of Bolívar and hero of Ecuador's independence, is buried. On the two other sides are hotels with arched arcades under which are little Indian shops selling all kinds of small trinkets, dolls and toys. Under the government building are more shops; at some of these children buy their books and school supplies.

The Plaza itself is full of flowers—all those we are accustomed to in our garden and tropical ones as well. Stiff little palms stand guard here and there. As we sit on a bench in the sun we are aware of an unusual sound, the constant soft shuffle of bare feet as Indian mothers and children cross the Plaza. That woman has a big bundle on her back, under her red shawl. As she nears us the bundle gives out shrill cries; it is a baby,

completely covered to protect it from the sun. For the midday sun, so near the equator, is hot and penetrating. Other babies, less covered, peer at us from their mothers' backs with their slanting eyes in wise little faces. Older children look at us seriously. We smile at them, and they are perfectly charming when their gravity breaks down and smiles ripple all over their faces like sunlight. All day long the pageant of Quito goes on. The bright reds, cerises, purples of the Indian costumes are dazzling. That little girl has just bought a new red felt hat at one of the small shops under the arcade; it makes a fine effect with her cerise dress! Those very clean Indians with large hats, red or striped ponchos, and short white trousers are from the village of Otavalo. There is a municipal swimming pool in that village and these Indians are the cleanest and most self-respecting in all Ecuador. They own their own land and have "factories" in which woollen cloth and rugs are woven.

Not all the people who pass are Indians. There are charming Ecuadorian girls in school uniforms or pretty dresses, and boys in white suits. The older women wear black, as do older women in Spain, with a black shawl over their heads. The younger women wear modern clothes, but many of them wear a lace *mantilla* instead of a hat. There are priests and monks of all types. We see Jesuits with their three-cornered black hats and Franciscans in their brown robes and sandals.

Look! Here comes a funeral. Except for its black plumes, the hearse is more like Cinderella's coach than it is like a funeral carriage. The horses are trimmed with gold and decorated with flowers, and on top of the hearse sits a golden angel.

Funerals here are pageants in themselves. We get a glimpse into a church in which the coffin is placed under a ceiling-high canopy of white and purple cloth streamers. Four life-sized angels cut from wood guard the four corners of the coffin. Somehow the words of an old rhyme keep going through my head:

"One to watch and one to pray
And two to bear my soul away."

But we are still interested in the Indians and we watch them go into a church near by. As they enter, the women hastily pull their shawls up to cover their heads. Many of them, as they go in, stop to kneel in the patch of sunlight that slants in the doorway, their hands held up in prayer. The dogs follow them and sit quietly in the cool church, or scratch their fleas.

Fleas! Quito teems with them, for the Indians neither wash nor change their clothing. In the narrow streets it is impossible to avoid brushing against the Indian women with their skirts wider than the sidewalks. Here is a group of three talking together, right under the sign which says: "Señorita, please do not get in people's way on the sidewalk; keep to the right." They stand there solidly; we push past them and at least three fleas leap from them to us. We wonder if it is good-neighborly to say much about them, but we discover that the people of Quito also joke about their fleas!

But we do not really mind about the fleas, at least we can keep our minds off them, for Quito is such a lovely city. It is almost as Spanish now as it was some four hundred years ago. The narrow, cobbled streets ramble up hill and down. Everywhere there are lovely old doorways and glimpses into gardens and old patios. Everywhere grow flowers—the Indians carry, and sell, big bunches of red carnations and white arum lilies.

Above the city rises Pichincha, Quito's own volcano, its lower slopes carefully cultivated and looking like a patchwork quilt in shades of green. It was on these slopes that General Sucre fought the Spaniards and gained independence for Ecuador. Beyond are the tall volcanoes; to see them one must climb to a little height. Sometimes the clouds roll away to show Cotopaxi's white crown. He looks quiet now, but in his day he was one of the angriest of all volcanoes and his roaring could be heard for many miles.

Of course we want to see how the Quiteños or people of Quito live; so we visit the residential district. There are some handsome mansions, some fine old houses, some delightful new ones. But the newest houses of all look like an architect's bad dream. Here is a Spanish-type house, next to it is an Eliza-bethan one, and next to that a Moorish creation. Why, in this beautiful old city must houses be like that? We are reminded of some suburbs of our own.

We are fortunate enough to see the inside of one of the more charming houses of Quito. It be-longs to the André Roosevelts, Americans who have lived in

Quito for a number of years. The house is a bungalow set in a garden where eucalyptus trees grow and flowers blossom all the year round. Inside, it is painted in gay colors and more color is given by pottery made by the Indians. On the wall of one room is a cactuslike Christmas tree, painted by Ludwig Bemelmans, who has written and illustrated so many amusing books for children and adults.

"Ludwig did that when he was staying here," Mr. Roosevelt tells us. "Ludwig has his own way of painting!"

On our way back to the hotel we find a small shop that sells "curios." Among the curios are several small, shrivelled black objects, no bigger than a doll's head. We know they are "shrunken heads" supposed to have been brought out of the jungle. We also know that they are not real shrunken heads but imitations, made to tempt tourists who seem to have a passion for such objects.

Real or not, we do not like these small heads, with their lips and eyelids sewed together, and would not feel easy travelling with them in their suitcases. But there seems to be so much told and written about the head-hunters of Ecuador that we want to find out if such people really exist. We have heard that they keep their enemies' heads as trophies, shrinking them to small size.

If they are real, we know that they live in the jungle, in a part of Ecuador over which Ecuador and Peru have lengthy disputes and even actual fighting. On the Peruvian map the territory belongs to Peru; on Ecuadorian maps it belongs to Ecuador. There is, therefore, a fine for taking a map from one country to the other.

We can't go into the jungle, so how can we find out about
the head-hunters? Fortunately we meet a young Colombian
who has been into the jungle to pan for gold, and he tells us
all about it. His story of his search for gold is so fascinating
that we almost forget about the head-hunters. He tells us
how snakes slithered away as he and his companion cleared leaves
and trees to bring the water of a stream
down where it was needed, when they
did not find gold right by the river's
edge. Mosquitoes sat so thickly on his
hands that he could scarcely weigh the
metal. In that part of the country gold
dust is used as currency. But our friend
didn't find so very much gold, and he
came out of the jungle with malaria,
and weak from blood-poisoning.

"The jungle is no place for a white
man," he says sadly.

Then we remember. "Did you meet
any head-hunters? Are there any? And
do they shrink heads, or doesn't the
government allow it?"

He laughs and shows us a photograph.
"This is a Jívaro Indian—what you call

a head-hunter. I lived with him in his hut for a few days, found him very friendly. When I came back he'd been killed by some of his enemies. Why, yes, they cut off his head. Perhaps they shrank it. Of *course* they still shrink heads if they want to, the government couldn't prevent it—but I don't think you'd call them head-hunters. I told you this man was very friendly. It just happened that some one took a dislike to him— and then——"

We don't care for shrunken heads, or most "curios," but we do find something wholly Ecuadorian that we think charming. In the market, Indians sell small earthenware figures painted in bright colors. They like especially to make figures for the Christmas crêche, as well as secular and amusing characters. Here are the Three Kings riding on their camels and wearing the most gorgeous robes, and here are Mary and Joseph and *el niño Jesús*. We see nothing like them in any other country, and we wonder how these Indians happened to make such delightful adaptations of religious figures. No one seems to be able to explain.

"Every one likes them—except perhaps the Ecuadorians, who think they are pretty ordinary," Mr. André Roosevelt tells

us. His own house is full of them. "Once a store in New York gave a big order for the figures; so we went to one of the men who makes them and we said, 'Make us ten thousand of these figures.' 'Ten thousand!' he said. 'Do you think I am going to spend my life making these figures?'" So no Ecuadorian crêches went to New York stores. So far the Indians have not gone in for mass production.

Take Panama hats for example. They are made in Ecuador and each hat is handwoven. They aren't really Panama hats at all, only called so because they were first sold in Panama. The Ecuadorian calls them *"Sombreros de Jipijapa,"* and he says they *aren't* Panama hats, hats made in Jipijapa *can't* be Panama hats. Incidentally, the material from which they are woven was used by the Incas to thatch their stone houses and comes from the *toquilla* palm.

* * * * *

A second morning the church bells awake us, and a third. One cannot listen to the bells of Quito without wanting to see some of the churches. Are they as harsh as the bells? They prove to be particularly fine. In Spanish days "the Quito school" of church decoration was famous. Most of the painting and carving was done by monks who had lived in Quito all their lives.

The most handsome of the churches is the Jesuit one of La Compañía de Jesús. We call it "the gold church," for it is gold from ceiling to floor. The main altar and those in the chapels are of solid gold; the walls and ceilings are of richly carved wood, overlaid with gold leaf. We are sure some of it must be Inca gold. There are places on the walls where the gold leaf has been scraped off by those who kneeled, pretending to worship; so now it is guarded carefully.

In contrast to the glittering church, we see an old, ragged Indian woman cherishing the most pathetic candle. It is nothing more than a wick around which she has folded a few tiny scraps of wax—these must be collected drippings from other candles. She begs a match from a man in the vestibule of the church and lights her poor little candle at one of the shrines. Her wrinkled hands tremble as she guards the precious flame from the draught.

*   *   *   *   *

Every one tells us we must see the equator monument, which is about half an hour's ride from Quito, at the spot where the equator passes through the country named after it.

Somehow we do not feel very enthusiastic. We see ourselves bent over school geographies, murmuring "The equator is an imaginary line—" But we hire a car and go.

The road is a cobbled one which takes us through Indian villages and up and down the steepest of hills. As usual our driver goes at breakneck speed, blowing his horn violently but not slowing down at curves. We expect to kill quite a few Indians, but somehow they get out of the way. The dogs, asleep in the road, scarcely bother to move; altitude makes them sluggish. We have no idea why we do not kill *them*, or the donkeys that also do not hurry.

Today the road is full of donkeys and Indian women carrying heavy loads. The men merely walk beside the donkeys, leaving most of the heavy work to the women.

The mountains are nearer now. Across the countryside tall eucalyptus trees march in endless rows.

The car comes to a stop and there is the monument. It is a marble shaft surmounted by a marble world, set in a bowl of desert land and surrounded by the wild, bare mountains. Never have we seen such coloring: some of the mountains are red, some are the deepest blue and purple, and above them are tall, white clouds. The sun, hot, bright, very close to us, glitters on the silver equator line that divides the marble world.

"The equator is an imaginary line—" But here it seems very real; it must be right under our feet! We almost expect to see a silver line like the one on the marble world.

"If you stand here on the steps," our driver tells us, "one foot will be in one hemisphere and one in the other." He stoops to pick a flower and hands it to us as a souvenir of the occasion. There are strange pretty little rock plants growing everywhere, but the one he has selected for us is a dandelion. Perhaps his choice was right; the other flowers were Ecuadorian, but the dandelion has a foot in each hemisphere.

From the equator our thoughts naturally turn to school; we have been eager to see the American School in Quito. There are a number of church and government schools in the city. Everywhere we see Indian children in blue aprons, and girls in the blue-and-white sailor suits that are the uniforms of the School of the Twenty-fourth of May (the day of Ecuador's independence). The American school has been open only a short while. It was needed because there was a German school, openly Nazi in its teachings. Now there are a hundred and sixty children of all nationalities in the American school, to which a Rockefeller grant has been given. Many of these children belong to prominent families of Quito; some are chil-

dren of the various consuls and government officials. Some are refugees from Europe.

The building is a low, rambling house, once a private residence. The charming old garden is now the children's playground; Pichincha looks down on it. Over the front door are the words: *Colegio Americano de Quito.* Many private schools are called "colleges" in South America.

The American principal shows us over the school. It is a busy and happy place, the work similar to that done in progressive schools in our country. Lessons are in English, with the exception of certain subjects required by the government of Ecuador to be taught in Spanish—notably the history and geography of the country. The first-grade children are learning to read in two languages. There are American and Ecuadorian teachers.

"Difficulty with all these nationalities—sixteen of them? No," said the principal. "Not the least difficulty with the *children* but some problems with the parents!"

We should like to see one of the schools to which the Indian children go, but there is not time. Airplane reservations cannot be changed; so we must leave the quaint streets and terracotta roofs of Quito. The fleas go with us.

Over the Desert to Peru

LIMA, CITY OF THE KINGS

THE FLIGHT to Lima begins over mountains; for a time
we fly through the "avenue of volcanoes" with huge
peaks on each side. In an hour we are down on the
seacoast, over Guayaquil. Guayaquil is a hot, damp
port in a country where all the rivers are in flood. Here the
Indian houses are built on stilts and stand right in the water.
As we fly over the muddy Guayas River we see long rafts
coming downstream. These rafts are made of the light balsa
wood which grows in Ecuador and they are bringing bananas
and cacao beans to Guayaquil. When the Spanish conquerors
came, they were met off the coast by Indians on balsa rafts
quite similar to these.

It is hot and sticky at the airport. Guayaquil has been
"cleaned up"—so we are told; no longer is it a pest-hole of
yellow fever and malaria. But this is the rainy season and
Guayaquil mosquitoes do not seem to know that, officially, they
no longer exist. They bite us fiercely and we are glad when it
is time to leave.

"Look your last at these green fields," some one tells us.
"Soon you will be seeing nothing but desert."

47

The change from emerald-green fields to sandy desert is like magic. We really do not know when it happens. Visitors who travel by ship down the coast of Peru and Chile sometimes grow tired of seeing nothing but desert day after day. In an airplane, one flies over the desert so quickly that it does not become tiresome, and from the plane one can see the bare mountains that rise like large heaps of gray-brown gravel behind the level desert. Sand and sand and sand, with nothing but a few scrubby cactus plants. Sand and sand and sand. Then we see tall shafts, the many hundreds of oil wells of Talara, important oil center and port of Peru.

We land in a mild sandstorm. Around Talara's airport are a few stiff Peruvian pines, even a few flowers planted in tubs sunk in the ground and carefully watered. We would not care to live here, but those who work in the oil fields have to do so, and there is a school for the children. Now that airplanes call at Talara, it is not so isolated, but before the airplane there were only ships, for there is no railroad.

As we leave Talara and fly over the desert, we try to think what it would be like to land there. Afterwards, in Lima, we did hear of a small single-motored plane which had to make a forced landing; food and water were dropped from another plane, passengers finally taken off, but captain and purser were lost in the desert where they wandered around looking for help.

Over more miles of sand, with small bumpy hillocks. We see some green spots carefully irrigated, with long irrigation ditches carrying water from the rivers that run down from the mountains to the sea. On this coast there is seldom any rain. When the trade winds come from the east coast, their moisture falls on the mountains as snow, and by the time they reach the coast they are perfectly dry winds. If clouds ever do get down to the sea the cold Humboldt Current keeps any moisture they may carry from falling as rain. Because of this, the coast of Peru must depend on irrigation for its water supply. The government controls the water and farmers pay so much to have a measured amount of water turned into the canals that irrigate their fields.

There are houses and streets and plazas below us now. Lima, Peru! It is a bigger city than we expected it to be. There is a thrill in coming to Lima, for it is our first large, modern South American city. We wonder how it will be like our cities, how it will differ from them. The land near the airport is dry and bare, but as we drive into the city there are handsome boulevards with trees and flowers. The pink and white oleander trees are in bloom. The grass is green, so green we can scarcely believe it. In summer time it has to be watered constantly, but in winter the fogs that hang over the city provide moisture.

Lima was one of the first cities built by the Spaniards in the New World. Pizarro, who founded it seventy-two years before the founding of Jamestown in Virginia, laid it out neatly in Spanish style, with buildings around plazas. Because it was founded on January 6, the day on which the Three Kings came to visit the infant Jesus, Lima was named the City of the Kings. It has always been called Lima, a corruption of Rimac, the Indian name for the river on which it stands.

The church bells of Lima are mellow and inviting. They lead us first to the twin-towered cathedral on the Plaza de Armas, the cathedral which Pizarro began to build. Out-

side the cathedral, Pizarro rides nobly on a prancing horse. Inside, he lies in a glass case, a shrivelled mummy, his heart in a glass jar near his feet. An American writer offended the people of Lima by calling Pizarro a "gangster" who had been given a place of honor in the cathedral. For, cruel and ruthless conqueror though he might be, Pizarro *was* the founder of Lima and through the years he has become a sort of hero to the people of his city.

As we come out of the cool darkness of the cathedral into the dazzling sunlight, the gathering of a crowd makes us hurry across the Plaza to see what is going on. Across from the cathedral is the President's palace, a handsome modern building. It is one o'clock and the sudden stir and bustle means the changing of the guard. The courtyard is full of soldiers, and, if the palace is handsome, so are the soldiers that guard it. Their uniforms are of black and red. Long tails of horsehair float from their shining brass helmets. Drawn swords glitter in the sun. We watch the ceremony, fascinated, and almost forget that the hot pavement is burning our feet through the soles of our shoes.

For Lima in the middle of the day is *hot*. On Jirón Unión, the main shopping street, hardly a soul is to be seen. From twelve to two shops are required by law to close; they roll down their shutters and the streets are deserted. About four o'clock in the afternoon a cool breeze comes up, the sun is not so fierce and the street is crowded with shoppers. We join them, and walk very slowly, for the windows full of Peruvian silver and fabrics woven by the Indians will not let us hurry. And, as no one else is hurrying, why should we?

A rug, woven by the Indians of Bolivia, pleases the artist especially. "Look at that exciting clash of color!" she says. "And look at that absurd bird wearing white galoshes! I must have it." When she buys it and spreads it on the floor of our hotel room everything in the room seems drab and colorless in comparison.

Here, in Lima, we begin to be conscious of Bolívar, and San Martín. Our hotel is on the Plaza San Martín and there is a large statue to the captain from Argentine. In the Plaza Bolívar, the great Liberator, rides a horse that is anchored to its pedestal by only two feet—Bolívar always rides a prancing horse, sometimes it seems to prance right off the pedestal.

"You should have seen that horse during the earthquake," a man who lives in Lima tells us. "I happened to be here and it suddenly became a rocking horse. How it stayed on the pedestal I don't know!"

Statues! They are everywhere in every South American city. Some are heroic, some are very small, some are good, some are bad. Our favorite in Lima is a group of llamas; it seems a friendly gesture for a big city to erect a statue to the animals that have been so useful to Peru. Another of Lima's friendly statues is that of Santa Rosa de Lima, patron

saint of Lima and of the New World. Rosa Flores was a
charming young girl who lived in Lima during the sixteenth
century. She was known for her faith and for her kindness
to the poor. Once, so the story goes, she saved the city from
an attack by pirates. When she was made a saint and her
statue arrived from Spain, it was met by the Viceroy of Peru
with pomp and ceremony, with lighted candles and processions,
and taken to San Domingo, where it is today. We are not surprised that the Limeños are so fond of Santa Rosa, she is
such a pretty little saint.

One of the things that is always interesting about a large
city is what it does for its working classes. Lima is proud to
show us. There are free hospitals for laborers and for babies.
There are many small houses which may be rented, and finally
owned, at very low cost, about five dollars a month in our
money.

In one part of the city we see the contrast between the old
and the new that is so much a part of Lima. A barefoot friar
guides a donkey laden with bags of rice to the gates of the old

Franciscan monastery. On
the pavement sits an old
Indian woman with many
small tin cans, which she
will sell for a few centavos
to the poor people who
come to the monastery
for food. They have been
coming here for nearly
four hundred years and

for all those years the brown-robed brothers have patiently handed out rice and beans and meat.

Directly afterwards we come to one of the Popular Restaurants, a shining modern place which serves meals for twenty to thirty centavos (three to five cents in our money). One room is especially for mothers with babies. Beside the tables stand pink and blue cots, and there are rows of bottles waiting for the babies. School children who would otherwise be undernourished get meals here twice a day; sixteen thousand of them are fed in the four Lima restaurants.

We go into the blue-painted kitchen to see the food prepared. There are huge iron cauldrons in which rice and beans are cooked, a hundred pounds at a time. Men are cutting up vegetables for soup. A meal at this restaurant consists of thick soup full of vegetables, meat, rice and beans, rolls, tea or coffee.

Yes, Lima is a mixture of old and new, but, damaged by the earthquake, the old will soon be gone. Some houses still have the shuttered balconies from which in the old days, Spanish women, not allowed to go on the streets, peered curiously at the life going on below them. The Torre Tagle palace, a fine old residence, has beautiful carved mahogany balconies and shuttered windows. Once llamas laden with silver came through the doorway and the silver was weighed in the huge scales that hung from the mouth of a ship's figurehead in the courtyard.

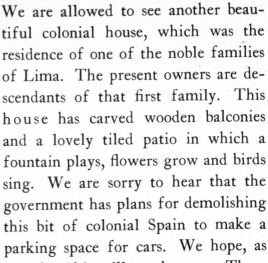

We are allowed to see another beautiful colonial house, which was the residence of one of the noble families of Lima. The present owners are descendants of that first family. This house has carved wooden balconies and a lovely tiled patio in which a fountain plays, flowers grow and birds sing. We are sorry to hear that the government has plans for demolishing this bit of colonial Spain to make a parking space for cars. We hope, as do the owners of the house, that this will not happen. There are so few old houses in Lima now, and so many modern buildings. Once the streets were lined by Spanish houses, their façades decorated with paintings of historical or Bible scenes.

Leaving the city, we drive out to see the suburbs, stopping at the handsome country club in Miraflores. Miraflores, overlooking the Pacific Ocean, is like its name, for there are flowers everywhere, and climbing geraniums scramble over all the walls. We see all that is left of the once lovely suburb of Chorrillos, almost completely destroyed by the earthquake. Now only a few walls stand and there are only ghosts of houses —we can see right into and through them. Poor Chorrillos!

When the cold damp fogs wrap Lima in its winter blanket, some of the Limeños go to find sunshine in a town in the hills above the city. Chosica is close up against the mountains and such cold, gray, rocky mountains they are, with no vegetation at all in some places and scrubby vegetation in others. They

54

would depress us, but to the Limeños they are beautiful. All around Lima are these bare gray mountains, and it is true that they have a beauty all their own. Around their bases, wherever irrigation ditches run, grow wild bamboos, so that each gray hill appears to be set in a saucer of green. Here among the mountains are the cotton fields. They grow a fine grade of cotton, one of the finest in the world, although the fields are watered entirely by irrigation. The Indians who work in the cotton fields live in the most temporary huts made of bamboo. In a country of little rain, four walls are a necessity; a roof may be considered luxury.

They say in Lima that in the summer it *never* rains, but the fact remains that sometimes the Limeños are surprised by a real rain. Then there is excitement, for some of the houses leak. One year, when the Humboldt Current suddenly changed its course, Peru had heavy rains and *then* there was trouble. In the country, adobe houses actually melted away. In Lima we hear of a family that had to sleep under the dining-room table to keep dry!

We find the Limeños friendly and hospitable. The city itself is friendly; while it is large, the shopping district, hotels, and many public buildings are centralized and it isn't hard to find one's way around. Pan-American Airlines has an excellent system in Lima. There is a "publicity man" who takes care of all visitors, finds out their interests, and, if they are not ordinary tourists, sees that they meet Limeños with the same interests. Through him we are introduced to a group of artists who are doing interesting work. One evening at half-past six, for tea time is late in Lima, we have tea at a charming studio club in a quiet tree-bordered square. There we meet artists and young people interested in writing. A poet gives us his book of poems translated from Quechua Indian into Spanish. Several artists take time to show us their paintings. Their only sorrow is that we cannot stay longer in Lima. "You North Americans hurry so!"

BURIED TREASURE

In most countries people *look* for treasure; in Peru they *find* it, for the country is a vast storehouse of treasure. Dry sand keeps its secrets for many hundreds of years; there is no moisture to rot the objects that are buried, no rain to wash them away. Something which tells more about the ancient Peruvians and their way of living is always being found.

Not so long ago, the owner of a cotton field decided to remove a mound of earth that was in the middle of the field. The *peon*, or workman, who was digging away the mound saw something shining. When he dug it out, the shining object was

a gold vase. There were other vases in the mound, undoubtedly ceremonial vases used in Inca or pre-Inca ceremonies, and they are now in the museum. The government claims all findings of this sort; the finder merely gets a small reward.

Near Lima are some fine pre-Inca ruins. First we visit the strange old city of Cajamarquilla. No one knows how old it is. Then we go to the ruins of Pachacamac. To get there, we drive along part of the Pan American Highway, which now runs from Lima to Santiago. At one side of us is the sea, at the other, huge sand dunes. We notice marks that look like ski tracks on the dunes and are surprised to learn that the sand is firm enough for skiing.

Many hundreds of years ago, people lived in the city of Pachacamac, in the house of sand mixed with water, a sort of adobe. There was a temple to the Creator God, Pachacamac, and all the peoples of the coast made pilgrimages to this temple. After a time the Incas, who were great conquerors, came down from the mountains and conquered these people. They built a Temple of the Sun on the hill above the temple of Pachacamac. In turn the Spanish came to Pachacamac, conquered the Incas, robbed their temples and threw out their gods. Years passed. Sand blew over the city and almost hid it. Archeologists dug out the ruins and they still stand. A heavy rain might wash them away.

As we walk through the ruins of this ancient city, the sun is blisteringly hot. We pick our way by ruined walls among open graves. Hundreds of people were buried here, and the graves were opened by treasure-seekers before the government forbade the public to dig in the ruins. Many bones lie on the sand.

Here is a long leg bone, there part of a skull and a wisp of red brown hair, a bit of burial cloth. "Do you think," I say to our guide, "that I could take just a *little* bone? It seems terrible to take one, but I'd like to."

He looks at me and laughs. "You'd better be careful. They say that it's bad luck. Once I brought a man here and he took part of a skull with him. When he got back to his hotel—" The guide's voice sinks to a whisper as if something very dreadful is coming.

"What?" I ask breathlessly. "What happened?"

"He had nightmares!" says the guide.

"Oh!" I say, disappointed. "Is that all?" And I cannot resist taking a bone, a very small bone. Because, after all, a nightmare is something one can take a chance with!

We climb to the Temple of the Sun, or to what is left of it. Sitting there on the crumbling terraces, we wonder how people lived in this dry, sandy place. There is no vegetation at all except for the gray-green air plants that grow on sand and rocks. Then we notice that beyond the ruins and beyond the sand

dunes is the river valley. Everywhere there are green fields, green because they are criss-crossed by irrigation ditches. The Incas and the pre-Incas knew a great deal about ways in which to make their barren fields fertile.

The fields of Peru owe much of their fertility also to guano deposits from the islands off the coast. These islands, some of which are near here, are the home of the famous sea birds, protected long ago by the Incas and now protected carefully by the government of Peru. Thousands of pelicans, cormorants and other birds live there. They eat the small fish brought by the warm Japanese Current, fish which die as they enter the cold Humboldt Current. As fish is good fertilizer, the droppings from the birds make the excellent and valuable fertilizer known as guano.

Under the sand at Pachacamac other buildings have recently been found. These are a great puzzle to archæologists for they are of *stone*, as are the ancient buildings high up in the mountains. There is no stone in this region, so where could these stones have come from? There are neat stone rooms with big stone baths that look like swimming

pools, and which are evidently ceremonial baths. Probably the stones came from the mountains. It is said that the Incas once took stones all the way from Cuzco to Quito, several hundred miles.

After Pachacamac, we visit the museums. At the Anthropological Museum, one room is full of mummies. There are shelves and shelves of them waiting to be unwrapped and studied by experts. Four hundred mummies were taken from one place. The people who live in a part of the country called Paracas used to bury their chiefs and priests most carefully. These mummies were found, well preserved, in the dry sand. A sketch on page 58 shows how a mummy, looking like a large mound, was found. Within the outer wrappings was a figure made to look something like a man, with a "face" made from strips of black cloth. This was dressed in the ceremonial robes of the dead chief, and in the museum we see those garments with exquisitely woven designs. Inside more wrappings was the mummy, or dried and shrivelled body, in a sitting position. Tucked under his legs and arms were bowls for him to take to the World of the Dead so that he might have food there. All kinds of things from jewelry to a pet parrot have been found buried with mummies.

These people were weavers, other groups were makers of beautiful pottery. Some of the early vases are in the shape of animals, many in the shape of llamas. One pottery llama is playfully scratching his ear with a hind foot; a pottery dog is gnawing a bone.

We have been so accustomed to seeing, in our own country, animals made into flower vases that at first we think automatically that these hollow animals must be flower vases. Most archæologists believe that they were filled with attractive offerings to the gods, and buried in the earth. If an Indian wanted his llamas to be healthy and increase, he buried one of these clay llamas in the field.

That night as we sit in our hotel room there is a deep rumbling, the room shakes.

"What *is* that?" we ask each other. The street cars always rumble as they pass, but this is a deeper rumble.

Again come the noise and the shaking.

"Probably the Inca coming to claim his bone," says the artist. "You were warned, you know!"

More rumblings and shakings. We realize suddenly that we are having a series of small earthquakes. They keep on for a while, then subside.

"Aren't you afraid of having another bad earthquake?" we ask some of our friends the next day.

"Why should we be? A bad earthquake comes to Lima only once in a hundred years."

AT THE FOOT OF EL MISTI

E FLY to Arequipa, second city of Peru, with a Cardinal and a baby. The Cardinal is American; the baby Peruvian. The Cardinal is making a good-will tour; with him are an archbishop, a bishop, and several priests. The baby is going with his mother and a very small sister to visit relatives in Arequipa. They sit quietly and solemnly, each child sucking on a rubber nipple, as many babies do in South America.

For the first part of the trip we are entirely concerned with the Cardinal; we have never seen such an important personage at close range. But after a time we become interested in the baby, for, when the little girl cries, the baby's mother suddenly plumps him into my arms. "Please, Señorita . . ." The baby and I are equally surprised. He stares at me with his big black eyes, then puckers up his face. Not approving at all of pacifiers, I hastily push the nipple of his a little farther into his mouth, and he sucks contentedly on it. We meet many small children in airplanes and they are almost always polite and well behaved.

As we near Arequipa we fly over a vast plateau. From this the tall mountains rise; and it is as if we had reached another world up here in the clouds. We can understand the story of the flood as told by west coast Indians. According to this, there came a mighty rain and the flood waters rose until they covered all but the tops of the highest mountains. Six people hid in the caverns in the mountains and, when the water receded, these six went down into the valleys and peopled the earth. Another version, more like our story of Noah's Ark, says that the six floated on a balsa raft until the flood subsided.

At Arequipa we, the baby, the captain, and the other passengers wait until the Cardinal's party have disembarked and been photographed. When the cheering crowd that greets them has gone, we can see the airport. The building is like a doll's house, white, covered with climbing geraniums and set here like a tiny oasis in a desert. For this place *is* an oasis on a broad, sandy plateau over seven thousand feet up in the Peruvian Andes. The air here is cool and invigorating; so some people from Lima use Arequipa as a holiday resort, and others come from the mining districts for rest and recreation.

Arequipa is an old Indian town, which later became a Spanish one, and it is still very Spanish. Its name means "Here we rest," and it was a resting place for the Inca runners who took messages from the imperial city of Cuzco to cities of the coast. It is seven thousand feet high, not enough to give us *soroche*. Above it tower three snow-capped, tremendous volcanoes: El Misti, "the Old Man," is the handsomest of these, for it is a single, perfect cone.

Almost all the houses in Arequipa, as well as its dignified

cathedral, are made of white volcanic stone. It is a picture-book city, white against a blue sky with palm trees growing in the central plaza and El Misti looking down on the cathedral. The doorways of churches and houses are richly decorated with carvings. The carvings are the only ones in which we have found Inca designs used along with Christian symbols; the mixture startles us. It is really quite natural, however, for Indian craftsmen were employed when the churches were built.

It is in the churchyard of one of the lovely old churches that we meet Carmencita. She is a little half-Indian girl, and she is busy picking flowers in the garden at the foot of the crucifix.

The crucifix is on the wall of the churchyard, and it, again, is very different, something one sees only in this part of Peru. It is a crucifix that was a Bible picture-book for the Indians who could not read. On the cross there is no figure of Christ, but many objects that tell the story of the crucifixion. There is a handkerchief with the imprint of Christ's face, the cock that crew when Peter denied his Lord, the pitcher and bowl to represent Pilate's washing of hands. There are the ladder, the hammer with which the nails were driven into the cross, the nails, themselves, the scourge and crown of thorns. We imagine a priest assembling the Indians around this crucifix and pointing out each object as he tells the story.

Carmencita is very busy. She fills a glass jar with water at an outdoor faucet, then she carefully arranges flowers. She cocks her head on one side critically, adds a rose here, a geranium there. Then she goes into the church, kneels a moment before the main altar, then carries her flowers to a side chapel.

This is Carmencita's week. The children of the church are each given a week to be responsible for the flowers. Carmencita takes her responsibilities seriously. Little Indian girls *do* take their responsibilities seriously and often those responsibilities are babies, heavy babies carried on the backs of too-small sisters.

An Indian baby in a long christening robe with pink ribbons is brought to the church to be christened. Will she grow to be as old as Carmencita, we wonder, or will she die, as so many Indian babies do, from disease or malnutrition?

Mrs. Bates, the American in whose charming pension, Quinta Bates, we are staying, tells us she has been godmother to over a thousand Indian babies.

"They almost all die," she says. "And the Indians aren't really sorry, for life is hard and Heaven is better. As godmother I have to supply the child's shroud and the little coffin. The parents always ask me for a yard of white ribbon. 'What do you do with that?' I asked them once. 'Oh, that ribbon hangs outside the coffin. It is a ladder for the godmother to climb to Heaven.'" She smiled. "I must have many ladders to Heaven!"

And she has other "ladders to Heaven" too, for in the years she has been in Arequipa Mrs. Bates has helped many Indians and their children.

In almost every book about South America the writer tells of Quinta Bates, for it's different from any other place. Quinta means "country house," and the house seems like a big, rambling country home, set in a lovely garden. Never have we seen so many flowers. Climbing geraniums grow to the tops

of the walls; there are hedges of scented geranium. Spring and summer and fall flowers grow together, chrysanthemums beside roses and forget-me-nots. Tall flowering trees give color everywhere. It is all the more remarkable when one remembers that this garden, like many other Peruvian gardens, depends on irrigation. Irrigation ditches run all along the edges of the bright green lawns. The ditches have a system of locks, so that the water level may be raised to flood one part of the garden at a time. We find comfortable chairs on the lawns and settle ourselves under a tree, only to find the water advancing over the grass towards us. We move on and settle down again, but in a few minutes the water follows us. So we walk down the path and out of the big gate into the street called the Calle Jerusalem. All the color, all the greenness has vanished, and there at the end of the street is the sandy desert. The garden seems more like magic than ever. Indeed, the whole setting of the *Quinta* is magical. We do not wonder that Noel Coward, when he visited here, wrote in the guest book,

> "Of every place I've been to yet
> This I shall leave with most regret."

We spend one day going to small villages outside of Arequipa. The road through the desert is walled with lava stone from the volcanoes; tall eucalyptus trees grow everywhere.

66

The smaller hills are of gray, bare stone; they look purple in the distance.

There are fertile valleys, well cultivated. Villages perch on the bare rock above the valleys, for the fertile soil is too valuable to be wasted by *living* on it. We stop in one village that is, without exception, the strangest and most different place we see in all our travels.

There is, of course, a small plaza with a church, and on the outer church wall are painted two large angels. A bell is being rung by a small boy up in the tower. Indian women come to Mass in calico dresses with bits of lace that pretend to be *mantillas* over their heads.

Scrambling up the hill behind the church are houses that are almost too strange to be true. They are *round* like African huts; there is a smoke hole in each mud roof, and each house is painted bright blue or yellow or pink. On all these, the three great volcanoes look down; we are quite near to them. From

the church comes a strange, primitive chanting. We go in. On the altar is a skull—and a live flame that, leaping, lights the darkness. We suddenly feel many, many miles away from civilization. This is one of the sudden and strange contrasts that makes Peru such a fascinating country.

Back in Arequipa we see a herd of llamas and follow them up the mountain to their village. In a courtyard they stand while their driver unloads the firewood twigs they have been carrying. Then the llamas nibble daintily at the stiff twigs as if they were quite a delicacy; for a llama does not mind coarse fare. We watch them and laugh, for they are such haughty, amusing creatures and have such funny ways of scratching one hind leg with another, or taking queer little mincing steps. They make a strange, complaining sound almost like the mewing of seagulls. Some of them have bits of bright-colored wool passed through holes pierced in their ears. In Inca days, there was a ceremony in which the ears of llamas were pierced for these colored decorations; today the decoration is the same as it was hundreds of years ago.

At festival times the sacred llama wore gold earrings! It would be interesting to note the number of Inca customs that survive among their descendants. A traveller in Peru a century ago noted that the Indians of that period used *quipus* or knotted cords such as the Incas used for keeping records, to keep track of their sins so

they might remember them all when they went to confession.

We have read how llamas spit when annoyed, and we wait for them to spit at their driver, who pushes them around none too gently. But, to our disappointment, not a llama is anything but polite. There are a few alpacas among them, with shorter legs and longer hair, but we do not see that other strange, more rare animal of the Andes, the vicuña. If we were going higher up in the mountains we should see many herds of llamas and alpacas.

It is Carnaval time while we are in Arequipa. For the three days before Lent begins, *Carneval* is celebrated in almost every city and town and village in South America. In Panama City and Rio de Janeiro there are big glittering carnivals. In tiny villages of the high Andes, Indians dye their llamas bright colors and trim them with ribbons. Arequipa has a smaller carnival than that of the big cities; we are fortunate to see it here.

"On Sunday," Mrs. Bates tells us, "the people have to behave, and you can go out. On Monday and Tuesday, things get pretty rough and it's best to stay off the streets. They squirt an etherized perfume that stings if it gets in your eyes and they throw flour and rice and corn along with the confetti."

On Saturday night at midnight, King Carnival is crowned in the Plaza. On Sunday afternoon we go down to the Plaza and stand on the steps of the cathedral to watch the Carnival parade. On the previous day, we saw one of the floats being made; a truck was being converted into a swan by means of a bamboo framework.

A crowd gathers with us on the steps. The Plaza seethes with people. All the arched windows of the pink buildings around the square are crowded with people. We are fascinated to see how many of the Indians have come down from the slopes of El Misti. They are in colors as bright as those we saw at Quito. The women and even some of the little girls wear stiff Panama hats with tall crowns and gay hat bands. In Ecuador, where Panama hats are made, the people wear felt!

Many little Spanish children are here with their Indian nurses; some of the children are in costume, clown costumes are favorites with the boys. No one is masked; masks are evidently not permitted on Sunday. People wear celluloid eye-protectors, because flour and rice *are* thrown in spite of the rules.

The Indians gather closer and closer around us. Mindful of fleas, we keep moving up another step, then give it up as hopeless. Some of the Indians are chewing coca leaves; it is said that the constant chewing of these leaves, from which cocaine is made, makes some of the adult Indians dull and slow-witted.

Here comes the band, and here come the floats! The first float represents the Incas, whose country this was, so many years ago. Against the background of a large Inca sun are Indians in Inca costume. Another float represents the colorful Indians of the Peruvian highlands. Then come pirates and comic figures. Last of all comes the Queen. She is riding in a swan—it is the float that yesterday we saw being made!

The floats turn off from the Plaza into a side street and the crowd begins to go home. We walk along the Calle Jerusalén behind groups of Indians walking slowly, because of the many children they have with them, towards their homes at the foot of the mountain.

El Misti looks down at the carnival doings with dignity. The white-haired old gentleman has seen many carnivals in his time.

OVER THE DESERT TO CHILE

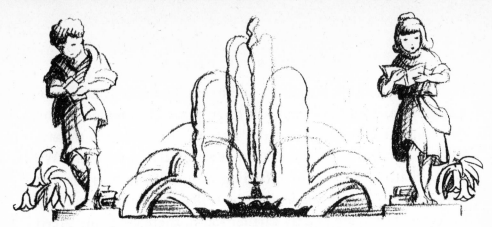

SANTIAGO DE CHILE

OVER THE DESERT and over the sea beside the desert to Chile! The Chilean desert is even more interesting and more beautiful than the Peruvian one, for there are more mineral deposits to give it color. We fly over a sea of cobalt blue, from which bare cliffs rise abruptly. At the top of the cliffs is a plateau, and behind this rises range after range of mountains in the most fantastic colors. Red, yellow, blue, purple; the kaleidoscope of colors fascinates us. Behind the colored mountains we see the snow-covered volcanoes, many of them with perfect craters.

It is only from the air that one can get a true idea of the strange Chilean coast. In this region are the rich nitrate mines, nitrate being one of the chief products of Chile. As we see small ports along the coast, we wonder how it would be to live in one of them. They are as bare and desolate as anything we have seen: nothing but sandy or rocky desert for miles with, every once in so often, the green ribbon of a river valley running down from the mountains to the sea.

Now we turn inland and land to refuel at an emergency station in the desert. Again one of those strange contrasts.

Here, with nothing but desert and bare mountains around it, is a modern airport building with huge plate-glass windows and furniture of chromium and red leather. Every one is thirsty, but the airport has nothing but lukewarm drinks to offer. We notice that the method of refueling isn't as modern as the airport—barrels of gasoline have to be rolled up to the plane.

As we start again and fly farther south, there are many green river valleys. This is part of Chile's fruit-growing section where melons, grapes, and other fruits grow.

The airport of Santiago is at the foot of the Andes. We wonder which city is more beautiful, Quito on the terraced slope of a mountain, Lima with its bare hills, purple in the twilight, Arequipa in the shadow of three volcanoes, or Santiago in the half circle of the magnificent range of the Andes. But the cities really cannot be compared.

There is no carnival going on in Santiago; it is prohibited here. The first thing we notice about the city is that it is something like Paris. And people move with a speed that surprises us, for we have been in the lazy tropics and in Lima, where no one hurries. We notice, too, that there are no Indians, no Negroes, and that the people of Santiago are fairer than any we have seen. Many of them have gray eyes—they are of mixed Spanish and English or Scottish descent. Also there is no tropical sun to darken skins, for Santiago has a moderate climate all the year round. Summers are not very hot nor winters very cold. Now we are in the part of South America where the seasons are opposite from ours. Here, far south of the Equator, it is March and the fall season. In Santiago asters and marigolds bloom in the gardens; leaves are falling from the trees.

Santiago is celebrating its four hundredth anniversary. We are sorry to have missed the pageant in which, at midnight, Pedro de Valdivia came riding into the city on his white horse, carrying on his saddle bow a small Madonna, as he did when he founded the city. We can still see the Madonna; she is in the old church of San Francisco. It was Pedro de Valdivia who gave Santiago its name—The City of St. James, patron saint of Spain. Another city, Valdivia, he named after himself. Valparaiso, chief port of Chile, has the most beautiful name of all for it means "Vale of Paradise."

Santiago makes us think of the old rhyme, "Tree on a hill, branch on the tree, nest on the branch, and the green grass grew all around." For in the middle of the city is a small hill, Cerro Santa Luciá, at the top of which Valdivia built his fort, at the foot of which the city first grew. On the hill there are flowers and trees and statues and grottos and fountains, and places to look out and see the view. There are castlelike buildings and little chapels, and at the top, a saint. Paths wind, stairs climb, and everywhere lovers walk two and two. From the top of the hill there is a fine view of the city and of the mountains that are so near. At sunset time the city seems to be set in a glowing, rose-colored bowl, for then the tall peaks reflect the sunset colors. Some years ago, a few citizens of Santiago found the Cerro just a bit too quaint and wanted to modernize it, but there were many

who cherished it with all its statues, its twists and turns and curlicues. So it remains as it is, which is a good thing, for there is nothing quite like it anywhere.

At the foot of the Cerro, two charming little statues, of a boy and girl reading, make us look across at the building they face. It is the National Library.

So we visit the Library and find there a children's room that surprises us, for the children are sitting at school desks and they seem to be studying. The librarian explains that this is because there are not many libraries in the schools. There is a bookcase of recreational books, but few of them are on the shelves: "The children like them so much that they are always in circulation."

We want to see more of the boys and girls of Santiago, and here we can visit schools. Summer vacation is over; it was not in Peru. We go first to the American school, a large school for girls called Santiago College. It is in one of the attractive residential districts, and to reach it we drive along the famous Avenida O'Higgins or Avenida de las Delicias, which runs for two miles through the city and includes many parks. O'Higgins seems a surprising name for the chief avenue of a Latin American city, but Bernardo O'Higgins, son of an Irish father and a Chilean mother, is the great hero of Chile. With the army of the Argentine general, José de San Martín, O'Higgins marched over the tremendous Andes Mountains to free Chile from Spanish rule. He became Supreme Director of Chile.

"How is it," I ask a Chilean, "that you honor O'Higgins so much more than San Martín? It was San Martín who organized the march over the Andes, wasn't it?" She looks at me as if I have asked a most foolish question. Then she says with pride, "San Martín was *Argentinian*; Bernardo O'Higgins was *Chilean*." O'Higgins had, of course, been working for the freedom of Chile before he joined San Martín.

On our way to Santiago College, we see many of the lovely parks. In one of the playgrounds the children play against a background of the Andes. Santiago College has handsome buildings and gardens. Over six hundred girls of several nationalities attend it. In their summer uniforms of pale pink, green, or blue, the girls look like so many flowers. The fact that so many girls go to the American school makes an amusing situation in Santiago; for many of their brothers go to English schools. The result is that in one family there may be a girl who speaks English with an American accent, while her brother speaks as the English do!

The artist sketches some of the girls at Santiago College; they talk to me while she is sketching. I ask a small, blue-eyed one about her nationality.

"I am Chilean!" she says proudly.

I question this.

"Well, my mother and father are English, but I was born in Chile; so that makes me Chilean, doesn't it?"

A number of the girls tell us where they have been spending the summer vacation. Some went to ranches, some to the sea-side resort of Viña del Mar, others went south to Chile's beautiful lake district. Almost all of them say they rode horseback, for Chile breeds fine horses and every one seems to ride. Nearly all of them say, "In vacation I had breakfast in bed," which seems to be a source of great delight. Both adults and children stay up late in Chile. Dinner at our hotel begins at half-past nine. By that time, we are usually starving; so we rush down to the dining room to find it "children's hour"; only a few children are at the tables as "early" as this.

From Santiago College we go on to the *Liceo Manuel de Salas*, which is a public junior-high and high school for both boys and girls. Although it is in a very old building, it is a most progressive school. The principal has studied in the United States and she is most interested in "the Good Neighbor Policy." She shows us some of the pictures made by her pupils for "The Day of the Americas" on which they had an exhibit representing the twenty-one republics. We see her Pan-American library with bookcases in which she intends to have books from all the American republics. We think it is a plan that schools in the United States might well follow.

"The books from your country are difficult for our boys and girls to read," she tells us. "They learn English, but not enough to read easily. We especially want a life of George Washington that they can read."

"And we should have a life of Simón Bolívar for *our* boys and girls," we say.

She nods. "You will have a good one some day, and we shall have lives of Washington and Lincoln. It will come."

THE COUNTRYSIDE

Our interest in the countryside begins with a visit to Señorita Mandujano at the Department of Agriculture. She is doing a remarkable piece of work with the *campesinos*, or country people, and her enthusiasm is contagious.

Chile has almost as difficult a problem with her *campesinos* as has Peru. True, in Chile the Indians are not so numerous nor so scattered. The fierce Araucanian Indians were never really conquered by the Chileans; they retired to the south where they live now, and they are recognized by the Chileans and given a voice in the government. But on all the *haciendas*, or large farms, all over the country, up and down the Andean slopes, there are many peasants who do not have much, if any, opportunity for education and who do not know the elements of hygiene. It is with these people that Señorita Mandujano works. She shows us the magazine that is sent out to thousands of peasants, and she tells how a family will sit up all night to read it. We are not surprised, for the magazine is most attractive. Each book has a different title and a bright picture on the cover. On one a Chilean cowboy looks across the fields, on another two *campesinos* are dancing the *cueca*. Inside, the magazine gives stories, bits of Chilean history, advice to farmers, elementary hygiene—and all in story form.

"The people write letters about their problems," she tells us. "Now they are writing stories for the magazine, and we can publish some of them. Look—" she brings out a huge stack of manuscripts, many of them written on wrapping paper. There are accounts of daily life, fairy-tales, poems—everything. "I am going to give them to the Library, for they are a perfect record of country life and Chilean folklore."

Thinking of the Indian babies of Peru, we wonder how many babies' lives are saved by Señorita Mandujano, who not only sends out the magazine but goes, with others, into the country districts and teaches the people.

Other books go out to the *campesinos;* there is a regular library service. Books are mailed to the people, who read them and return them free of charge. The books are children's classics—*Gulliver's Travels, Pinocchio, Don Quixote,* and others. The need is for simple adult books.

"Do they take care of them?" we ask.

In reply, Señorita Mandujano reads us a letter from a countryman who says: "If you can find a single spot on the beautiful books you lent me, you may excommunicate me."

When we drive out into the country to see something of it

and of the vineyards, we are especially interested in the *campesinos* and how they live. Here is a neat adobe house, with a grape arbor under which the whole family, including the baby, is having an outdoor meal. There is a cheerful red-checked tablecloth on the table. Are these readers of the magazines, we wonder? But on the whole, the people look happier than many we have seen. The climate of Chile is kind; life is not so difficult. The people do not own their own houses, and they work for small pay. It has been this way for generations. Some day there may be social legislation to remedy this condition.

We are going to one of the largest vineyards, *Hacienda* Santa Rita, and it is quite a long way from the city. The dusty country roads go through orchards and fruit farms; we see many high, mule-drawn wagons piled with watermelons. Everywhere there are the tall, slim poplars so typical of Chile, and, where there is water, the largest and "weepingest" willows we have seen. In this part of Chile, there is rain during only about three months of the year, but the land is well irrigated by mountain streams.

As we come near Santa Rita, we see the vineyards stretching for miles against a background of mountains. The superintendent takes great pleasure in showing us around. Unfortunately, grape-picking has not begun; it starts next week. He takes us to see the presses that press out the juice of the grapes. From there we go into cellar after cellar where wine is ageing in huge wooden casks. There are up-to-date concrete containers into which the wine goes at first, but it must age in wood. He points proudly to the dates on the barrels, showing how long the wine has been "in wood." Some of the cellars are the old, vaulted ones built by the Spaniards.

We go into the bottling room, where the bottles are being corked or capped by up-to-date machines. All down one side of the room silver-foil sparkles on the tops of the white wine bottles; on the other side, the tops of the red wine bottles shine red. Girls are busy pasting Santa Rita labels on the bottles.

We see the old mansion with its lovely gardens. In one of the gardens is the statue of a saint, evidently a farmer-saint, for he holds a spade. When the weather is unusually dry, the people come in procession to pray to this saint for rain.

As we leave Santa Rita, the superintendent gives us eight bottles of a fine white wine. We had heard that vineyards gave visitors a bottle of wine, but Santa Rita is even more generous. We can't possibly drink it all before we go on to Argentina, and we can't take it in our already crowded suit-cases. So we have to find ways of sharing it. The best Chilean wine compares favorably with European ones. Chile uses her grape juice in every possible way. We have unfermented, green grape juice served at breakfast instead of orange juice.

Over the Mountains
to Argentina

THE GREAT MOUNTAINS

ONE MORNING we wake with a feeling of excitement, a feeling that this is the most eventful day of our journey. It is the day when we are to fly over the mountain wall of the Andes on our way to Argentina. There is a railroad through the mountains; part of it is now blocked by an avalanche and the trip must be completed by automobile. The journey from Santiago to Buenos Aires takes two days by train, only five hours by plane.

The flight over the Andes, or rather through the Uspallata Pass between the highest volcanoes, was once considered the most dangerous in the world. Aviators died attempting it. Now the commercial planes cross several times a week, but they are always careful not to attempt the flight in bad weather. There are constant radio reports from the station in the middle of the Pass. We have heard tales of passengers going to the airport for three or four days in succession and finding the weather unfavorable and the flight postponed. The plane may even go up, find clouds in the Pass, and return to the airport. But we are fortunate; the weather is perfect. We leave at dawn from the airport that is only twenty miles away from the mountains. We know that in half an hour the plane must be flying over the Pass at fifteen thousand feet and wonder how it can be done.

We take off. The plane rises steeply and sharply, and, as we rise, we can see clearly the mountains over which we are to go. Range after range, each higher than the other, with the snowy volcanoes forming the crest. We do not have to fly over the highest ones; the Pass lies between them.

Over one range, over another. These are far more impressive than any we have seen.

By each seat there is a slender rubber tube attached to a tank of oxygen. The tube has a bone mouthpiece, at present carefully covered with cellophane. The steward shows us how to control the oxygen supply by pressing a button, and how to take the oxygen by nose or mouth. At fifteen thousand feet, some of the passengers feel the need of oxygen, others do not. Every one experiments with it, and little hisses come from all over the plane as the passengers press buttons and oxygen escapes.

Now we are flying through the Pass. On one side rises the giant Aconcagua, 23,000 feet high, its top hidden by clouds. There is a strong wind up here and on many days Aconcagua flies a scarf of snow miles long. On the other side is Tupungato, its snowy summit standing out clearly.

The captain comes through the plane and talks to the passengers. He tells us that the flight is really more beautiful in this season, when there is little snow on the mountains and one can see the beautiful colors of the rocks.

We shall not see again in our lifetimes anything as majestic as we see here at the crest of the Andes. The lower mountains, on which we look down, are reddish brown and the formation of the rocks on their sides looks like a marching band of brown-clad figures—they are called "the monks." In some places the rocks are deep red. In the distance the mountains shade from blue into purple.

We have flown over many mountains before; they lay beneath us quietly, like sleeping animals. But these mountains are not quiet and they do not sleep. They reach their great, jagged peaks up into the sky and seem angry that we, in our small silver plane, dare to disturb them. We think of Lord Dunsany's play, *The Gods of the Mountains*, and of the awesome moment in that play when the gods of the mountains are heard offstage, but not seen. These *are* the gods of the mountains, we feel their presence but we are not afraid.

At one time the right wing of the plane seems almost to touch one of the peaks, the left another. We know that these peaks are perhaps two miles away; the clear air makes them seem nearer. But we can see why a plane does not go through the Pass in heavy clouds.

The purser says, "We are flying over the Christus." We look down and there, very small, very far below us, is the Christ of the Andes. This famous statue, made from cannon melted down, was placed here after a border dispute was settled by Chile and Argentina without war. One hand is raised in blessing, the other holds a cross. On the base of the statue are the words: *May these mountains crumble into dust before the peoples of Argentina and Chile break the peace which they have sworn to maintain at the feet of Christ the Redeemer.* We say the statue was "placed here," but seeing it helps us to realize the tremendous difficulty of transporting it to the high Andes. Part of the way it was pulled by mules, the last part of the way it was moved by thousands of soldiers and sailors. To settle a border dispute in this way is an event in South America, where wars have grown easily over disputed territory. Perhaps some day a statue will mark the settlement of the long border argument between Ecuador and Peru.

Look! Ahead of us is a huge, rocky wall; we are steering straight towards it. Another half minute— But the plane banks, makes a sudden sharp left turn and we are flying down a valley.

Now that the plane is descending, some of us feel sick and dizzy, for it is hard on the human system to go up fifteen thousand feet and down again in an hour. Panagra says that since we crossed the equator we are condors, but at fifteen thousand feet I am sure I am *not*. I begin to feel very strange, part of me seems to be floating in space. I look back at the artist, who is sitting behind me, but she is talking cheerfully with the captain and not even thinking of the oxygen tube. Then I look at the *Señora* from Chile who sits across the aisle. She has turned the lovely greenish color that I *feel* and she is taking oxygen. So I take some, too. It has only a slight odor, as I breathe it in things do not swim around me quite so much. But, in spite of the oxygen, the rest of the descent is a jumble in my mind— We shall be down soon—how sick I feel!—the colors are lovely—but it's better with the eyes closed—I wonder if I look as green as she does—a little more oxygen might help —I'm really going to be sick—oh—here we are! A deep sigh of relief and I totter weakly from the plane. We have landed

in Mendoza, center of the grape-growing district of Argentina.

In the lower altitude of Mendoza I soon begin to feel better, and the *Señora* is no longer green. The artist and I walk to the back of the airport and look across the plains to the tremendous range we have just crossed. We wonder how they seemed to José de San Martín as he spent months here preparing his army for the march over the Andes. There must have been many days when he looked across to those white peaks and wondered whether he and O'Higgins and their brave little army would ever get safely to the other side. Courage must have run high when San Martín, coming from the cathedral bearing the flag that had been blessed, met his soldiers in the plaza and urged them on with his famous speech.

"Soldiers! this is the first banner of independence that has been blessed in America. Swear, as I do, to uphold it and die in its defence."

"We swear!" shouted the voices of ten thousand soldiers as the blue-and-white banner floated out above them. In his heart each man must have known what lay ahead. Steep paths, rocky precipices, deep gorges, cold, hunger, mountain sickness—death for almost half the army. With the picture of those wild, rocky peaks clear-cut in our minds, we do not wonder that San Martín's march over the Andes is counted one of the great achievements of history.

Shortly after leaving Mendoza, we fly over low hills, but most of the way is over the *pampas* of Argentina. Smoothly, steadily, we go over mile after mile of level country. Somehow we had pictured a flat green or

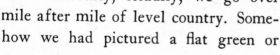

brown plain with herds of cattle grazing here and there and scattered ranches. We can see the cattle, looking like clusters of brown coffee beans; we can see the *estancias*, ranch houses with their red roofs. A long line of cattle and men is stringing out along a road. The men are *gauchos*, or Argentine cowboys. We wish we could see them at closer range, though we know the *gaucho* is no longer as picturesque as he used to be. In the old days *gauchos* were practically born in the saddle. When a baby was only a week old his father or brother galloped with him over the pampa until the infant cried and had to be returned to his mother. This was repeated many times so that the "little *gaucho*" would get the feel of the saddle. As soon as he was old enough he rode a quiet horse. But the *pampa* from the air! *That* is a surprise. It is truly the flattest plain we have seen, but it is not the never-ending sea of grass we had pictured it. It unrolls beneath us like an inlaid linoleum, with squares and oblongs of vivid green, sand yellow, dusty purple, all fitted together like a picture-puzzle. Trees show where there are houses, and through the bright colors of the picture-puzzle curl long, winding rivers. If we were on ground level, the picture would be different and far more monotonous, for each of the colored "inlays" is really very large. The *estancias* would astonish us by their size. A large one may have a hundred thousand acres of land. More than five hundred workers may live on one ranch.

The airport at Buenos Aires is thirty miles from the city. As we drive between fields, the vegetation looks more like that of the United States than any we have seen. It is March, we remind ourselves, but the fields are full of goldenrod and asters.

THE CITY OF GOOD AIRS

WE ARE coming into the city. What will Buenos Aires be like? We wonder about this huge, modern city that we have heard of as "The Chicago of Argentina," "The Paris of South America," "The Queen of the Silver River." Chicago—Paris—London —is Buenos Aires really like all of these? Has she no personality of her own?

We find, almost at once, that Buenos Aires *has* a very definite personality, and one that we like. Perhaps this may be a little more difficult to find than that of Quito or Lima or Santiago, but it is there for those who care to look for it.

Here on the outskirts of the city, we see, among the modern trolleys and buses and autos, the most astonishing carts. Big high-wheeled wagons with designs painted on them, drawn by three or four horses, are returning to the country after taking produce to the docks. Small, very gaily painted milk carts are drawn by horses in brass-decorated harness. They are driven by men in black berets, Basques from the Basque country of the Pyrenees.

School is out for the day, and the streets are alive with children. Boys and girls alike wear the white, box-pleated coat-apron that is the school uniform of Argentina. The girls wear big bows of white or colored ribbon on their hair. Bright school bags, red and green and blue, are slung over shoulders. The policeman in his high, white traffic tower stops traffic so that children may cross the street. This is really necessary, for there are few stop-and-go lights and traffic seems to move continuously and very fast. We never really learn to cross the streets of Buenos Aires with dignity but scuttle across them like frightened rabbits. The system the Porteños, or people of the city, seem to use is to ignore oncoming cars and start across, forcing the cars to stop. But this takes more courage than *we* have.

One of the first things that gives the City of Good Airs personality for us is the story of how it got its name. In Spain, there was a painting known as "The Virgin of Good Air," in

which a stately Virgin is shown taking mariners under the shelter of her robe. Beneath the clouds on which she stands lies the sea, dotted with sailing vessels large and small. It was to this Virgin that sailors prayed for fair weather before leaving for adventures in the New World. So, when after being storm-stayed, Pedro de Mendoza, the founder of the city, was finally brought to it by favorable winds, he named it "The City of Our Lady of Good Air." A copy of the painting was later presented by Spain to Buenos Aires.

In the center of the city we feel a little lost. Again the personality of "B. A.," as South Americans call it, seems hard to find. But we won't let it down us. So we make a list of all the things that are, on the surface, Buenos Aires:

Traffic.

Wide streets, the Avenida 9 de Julio is the widest avenue in the world.

Parking spaces for cars. That under the Avenida holds hundreds of cars.

Uncrowded, modern subways.

Parks—the most magnificent to be seen anywhere.

Skyscrapers.

Modern comforts of all kinds.

But still we haven't found the things that make B. A. different. How would we go about it in our own cities of New York and Philadelphia?

First of all, the heart of the city. In New York, it would be Times Square or Rockefeller

Center; in Philadelphia, Independence Square. In Buenos Aires, it is Plaza de Mayo which is really Independence Square, for the monument that marks Argentina's independence is there and the date is May 25. It is a large plaza, with handsome, patterned gardens. At one end is the Casa Rosada, or Pink House, in which the President lives. What city but park-minded Buenos Aires would have set a pink palace in a park in which the walks are of pink gravel to match the palace? And at the palace gates are guards in colorful uniforms. Opposite the Casa Rosada, the statue of San Martín on his bronze horse looks across at the guards who wear the uniform of his own army of the Andes. In the olive-green cathedral with its Greek pillars, San Martín himself sleeps. What city but Buenos Aires has a green cathedral? The most interesting building of all is the Cabildo, or council house, with its arches and towers, one of the few really colonial buildings of modern B. A. It was at the Cabildo, on a rainy May 25, that the independence of Argentina was proclaimed.

We wonder if anything more of old Buenos Aires remains, and find very little. Even the Cabildo lost part of itself when the streets were widened. What is there left to remind us of the tiny settlement that, withstanding great dangers from fierce Indians, became the fourth city of the world? Very little, except a tall shaft that marks the spot where the city was supposed to be founded.

It doesn't seem possible to believe that only a little over a century ago, a traveller wrote of Buenos Aires—"In this country the atmosphere is moist and spoils the furniture, especially at Buenos Aires where the floors of rooms exposed to the south are always damp, the walls are covered with moss and that side of the roof is overgrown with thick grass nearly three feet high." It goes to show how rapid and spectacular the development of the city has been. (The south side of the house is, of course, below the equator, the side that gets least sunshine.)

A city's shops always tell us something about it; so we go to Calle Florida, the main shopping street. This *is* different; it isn't like the shopping district of any other city. For Calle Florida is closed to traffic and pedestrians may use the whole street. At first, from force of habit, we cling to the narrow sidewalks; then we find it more comfortable to walk in the street. Browsing around the shopping district, we find many bookstores. On the counters we see the dignified faces of the Liberators looking at us from many books. Cheek by jowl with them are Mickey Mouse and Donald Duck! There is even a street vendor of children's books; children and their parents cluster around him. The English Bookshop is quite as English as its name, and full of mothers and children buying books; there is a large British group in B. A. We have seen many young Porteños who go to English schools; we know them by their gray flannel uniforms. There are people from many countries in Buenos Aires; it is a most cosmopolitan city.

One shop that fascinates us is a large one which carries schoolbooks and supplies. Here are the red and green and blue schoolbags that we have seen children carrying. What will go into these schoolbags, we wonder? Dull schoolbooks with rather uninteresting pictures? To our delight we find a counter that fairly glows with color. The covers

of Argentine readers would encourage any child to read; they
are printed on boards in the brightest colors. "But," we say to
ourselves, "there will not be color pictures inside." There *are*
—and very gay ones. Even the history books have colored pictures. There is a great deal about patriotism, the country, the
flag; young Argentinians are certainly taught pride in their
big, progressive country.

Perhaps nothing gives us more of the personality of a country than its schoolbooks. The big city takes so much of our
time we can't visit schools; so we are glad to see the books.

It is funny that we, accustomed to large cities, should make
the mistake of underestimating the size of Buenos Aires. We
get into a taxi and ask to be driven to the Palermo Parks. The
taxi goes on and on; our bill goes up and up. For the Palermo
Parks are magnificent and amazing—and endless. They include
lovely gardens, lakes with swans, statues of every kind. They
also include the Botanical Gardens, the race-track, the zoo!
So one can scarcely expect to cover them in a brief time.

Again we feel lost in this city; again small things that en-
dear our own cities to us make us feel at home in Buenos Aires,
though here the small things are different. There are the lovely
street flower-stands—we buy two dozen roses for twenty-five
cents. There are the fruit shops with melons all done up in
colored paper frills, and the small shops that sell birds in cages.
There are the gay toylike milkwagons that we saw before.
And, after all, Buenos Aires can't make us feel she is *all* dignity,
for she is still dressed for the Carnival—in the Plaza de Mayo,
we see the gigantic figure King Carnival himself, and down
the wide streets are decorations of huge Carnival figures!

We rise very early on the morning that we leave Buenos Aires and drive through the city and its outskirts in the darkness. It is four o'clock on Sunday morning; the cafés are busy, the streets full of life. We are sure the Porteños *never* go to bed. Young people are returning from after-carnival parties; it is quite startling to see the glow of almost every street light fall on groups of gypsies and pirates, soldiers and flower-girls.

We start our flight in the darkness. As our plane takes off, the purser says, "Turn off all the lights in the plane and look down."

"Why," says a passenger. "It's the sky turned upside down!" For our last view of B. A. is a magnificent illumination. The city being perfectly flat and laid out symmetrically, we can see miles and miles of street lights twinkling like stars in a regular pattern below us. Again we have a sense of the great size of the city. We have only *begun* to find the personality of Buenos Aires. To know it we must come back—and stay.

Over the Rivers and Forests to Brazil

THE BUSY CITY OF SÃO PAULO

N OW WE are on our way to the last and largest South
American country that we shall visit. We are flying with the company that serves the east coast,
Panair do Brasil, but still in the big Douglas plane
to which we have become accustomed.

We fly in the semi-darkness across the La Plata River, and
over the small but progressive republic of Uruguay. We look
down at what we can see of this little country and are thankful
that, somewhere in the world, a small neighbor can live peacefully between two big ones. There was a time when Brazil
and Argentina each tried to absorb Uruguay, but they have
learned to respect her.

The dawn is different from any we have seen. This one
literally "comes up like thunder." Beneath us is a floor of dark
gray clouds; tremendous, frightening storm clouds billow in
the sky. The storm breaks; there is a blinding rain and a strong
head wind.

Our first landing is at the airport of Asunción, capital of
Paraguay. The tropical rain is still coming down in sheets;

our brief view of Paraguay is an impression of native huts, coconut trees, red-clay roads, and a dripping greenness. We sniff the air appreciatively, for it is the first time in a month that we have smelled damp earth.

When we start again, the air is very rough. We are flying over the jungle, a jungle in which there are strange swamps, a green jungle made even greener by the rain. The next airport is a complete surprise. It is at Foz do Iguassú (the Falls of Iguassú), where Brazil and Argentina and Paraguay meet. The landing field is high in waving grass. The "airport" proves to be two tents, canvas over bamboo poles. There, because we are crossing the Brazilian border, we go through the usual passport and customs formalities. Brazil is kind to visitors, everything is made easy for us, and we do not even have to open our suitcases for the customs officials. Every one from Foz do Iguassú is assembled to watch the plane come in, we even see some *gauchos* with their long baggy trousers and pleated leather boots. Brazil also has her pampa and her cowboys; we are apt to think of them only in Argentina.

The purser tells us that the pilot will fly low over the Falls, so that we may see them. He flies *very* low, circling the Falls completely. The Falls of Iguassú are one of the natural wonders of the world. Set as they are, in the heart of the jungle, it takes a long time to reach them by boat or train. We are fortunate to see them from the air even though we cannot hear the roar of the waters. In a gorge that is two miles wide, more than seventy cascades, some large, some small, leap over the rocks, sending clouds of spray many feet into the air. It is a superb waterfall, higher than Niagara, wider than the Victoria

Falls in Africa, and it fully deserves its Indian name of Iguassú
—Big Waters.

Before we reach São Paulo, first industrial city of Brazil,
we fly low over the coffee country. Coffee did not grow in
Brazil originally, the plants were brought from French Guiana,
more than two hundred years ago. Now Brazil produces more
coffee than any other country in the world. The coffee trees,
with their dark green leaves and red berries, thrive on the rich
soil of the hilly regions of the state of São Paulo. We are in
a country that has states like our own. Twenty states and one
federal district make up the United States of Brazil.

The coffee farms, or *fazendas*, are lovely to look at. The
soil is bright orange-red in striking contrast to the green trees.
The roofs of the houses, with tiles made from the red clay of
the district, match the soil exactly. We can see the big houses,
with rows of smaller ones for the workers. Near the houses
are the huge drying grounds where the coffee beans are spread
out to dry in the sun. The big coffee farms are villages in themselves with their own shops, electric light and telephone sys-
tems. Some are very up-to-date and provide
excellent homes for their workers; others give
their workers rather poor homes. There are
more than forty thousand coffee farms in the
state of São Paulo.

Brazil gives its coffee good publicity. It is served at every airport
as the Brazilians drink it, in tiny
cups and very black, with much
sugar. The calendar put out by the

National Institute of Coffee quotes the Frenchman, Talleyrand:

Coffee should be black as the devil, hot as hell, pure as an angel, sweet as love.

And that is just how Brazil serves it! It takes North Americans as long to get used to Brazilian-made coffee as it takes Brazilians to get used to the way we make it.

In a cloud of red dust, our plane lands on the red soil of São Paulo airport. The big airport is full of color and gaiety. Dozens of Paulistas, or people of São Paulo, are here to meet the plane. They are all in bright, summery clothes. One of the things we notice about the friendly and social Brazilians is the number of people who meet or see their friends off at airports. One traveller by plane will be "seen off" by twenty or more friends. When it is time for the plane to leave, there is a perfect flutter of good-byes and much friendly chatter. Women kiss each other fervently; men give each other the embrace that we have seen them give everywhere in South America, but especially here. Each man puts his arm half way around the shoulders of the other and they pat each other enthusiastically on the back. Children are kissed and hugged by the grown-ups; they in turn kiss the hands of older people.

Along the red roads, by red fields, we drive to São Paulo. With our entrance into a Brazilian city comes a change of language from Spanish to Portuguese. Saint is no longer *San* but *São*. A square is no longer a *plaza* but a *praça*. A street is no longer *calle* but *rua*. Some words are the same in the two languages; some are very different. Newspaper headlines suddenly seem strangely exclamatory:

O PRESIDENTE ROOSEVELT

we read, but realize that "o" is only "the"!

São Paulo is a city of parks, of tall palm trees, of wide avenues and skyscrapers. It is a city that has grown and is growing rapidly. "A new house is built in São Paulo every half hour," they tell us proudly. The center of the city, "the Triangle," is the only remaining bit of old São Paulo. Here the streets are narrow and are open only to pedestrians.

One thing that we like about São Paulo is its avenues of flowering trees. Trees that flower in the spring and fall are planted alternately. Now, with the fall season beginning, the streets are golden with acacia blossoms. In the spring they will be blue with the flowers of the jacaranda tree. There are flowering trees and lovely gardens everywhere, especially in the fine residential district known as the American Garden. Here the streets bear the names of all the American republics, Mexico Street, Argentina Street, and so on.

São Paulo guards the most sacred spot in all Brazilian history, the battlefield of Ipiranga. It was there that Dom Pedro I, Emperor of Brazil, tore the colors of Portugal from his hat and threw them to the ground shouting, "Independence or death!" The spot is marked by an enormous and dignified monument and by the Ipiranga Museum. It is interesting to think that three emperors actually reigned in America.

Once the place on which the city stands was primitive jungle. A little piece of it still remains to show us what the country used to be. In the "Jungle Park" the tall trees with intertwining creepers and many parasites still grow. It is in this park that we see a man spearing dead leaves with a pole on the end of which is a sharp spike. Very deliberately he spears one leaf and then another.

"It must take forever to get all the leaves up *that* way!" we say to the Paulista who is with us. In our efficient and hurrying North American way, we feel we must *do* something to speed up the process.

But the man who lives in São Paulo smiles at us. "There isn't any hurry," he says. "Not many leaves fall here, you see." And we suddenly realize that this is true and that the leaf gatherer has only a few leaves to contend with. Even though this is a busy city, life is leisurely. There is "no need to hurry."

       *   *   *   *   *

While we are in São Paulo we go to visit the Snake Farm at Butantan. This was the first institute for the production of snake-bite serum in the world, and it has been used as a model by other countries, including our own. The need for it in Brazil was great; each year thousands of people died of snake bite. Now many lives are saved by the serum made at Butantan and sent to farmhouses all over Brazil and to other countries as well.

We are surprised to find Butantan such a beautiful place. The buildings, with their weathervanes in the form of coiling snakes, stand in a handsomely planted park. The snakes have their own houses. Here they are, in two deep, enclosed pits. In the one by which we are standing there are about six houses, like small Eskimo igloos, made of red clay. The houses stand in the shade of a lovely jacaranda tree.

Some of the snakes have retired to their houses, others are

slithering over the ground. The attendant says he will show us how the venom from which the serum is made is taken from the snakes.

The snake selected is a big rattler. The man in charge pins it down with a forked stick. It lashes from side to side and rattles angrily. After quite a struggle, the expert grasps the snake just behind the head and forces its jaws open. We look down into the ugly, toothless mouth. The snake lashes fiercely with its tail.

"Has the man ever been bitten?" we ask.

"Yes, about seventeen times. When he is bitten, he takes the serum. But he is very skillful in handling the snakes."

The attendant is holding a shallow glass container under the snake's mouth. Drops of venom fall from the angry mouth into the container. And all this time the man is calmly smoking a cigarette.

"Each one of these drops can kill ten men," he says, smiling up at us.

Then he releases the snake, which glides sluggishly away. The venom will now be injected into a horse. The blood of the horse will set up an immunity to the poison, helped by an

injection of serum. The new serum is then made from the horse's blood. We see a corral full of horses used for making the serum, and we don't envy them.

Snakes are sent to the Institute from all over the continent. People who live in the country catch the snakes, put them in boxes and mail them to Butantan. In return they receive serum, one serum for each type of snake common to the district, and a general serum to be given to a person who does not know what snake bit him. A man who is bitten hurries to the nearest farmhouse to get serum. If he can, he takes the snake—harmless for a time after biting—with him, and it is sent to Butantan.

We are taken next to see the non-poisonous snakes which are kept in a separate enclosure. There are some pretty ones here, and a baby boa constrictor, which coils itself around the attendant's arm. He explains that the difference between types of snakes is that poisonous ones have no teeth, while non-poisonous ones have; the young of poisonous snakes are expelled from the body of the female alive; non-poisonous snakes. lay eggs. The non-poisonous snakes kill harmful insects and are sent to farmers who would like to have them. This boa constrictor kills poisonous snakes, so is a good "pet" to have around a farm.

In the museum, there are exhibits that curdle our blood. Plaster casts of legs show the effect of snake bite with and without the use of serum. Preserved in bottles are all kinds of snakes, poisonous spiders, centipedes, and scorpions.

Brazil is putting up a brave and constant fight against diseases and other dangers of the tropics. The mosquitoes that carry yellow fever and malaria have been almost eliminated from the towns, but there is now a new enemy to fight. A small but deadly mosquito came riding on planes from Africa and settled itself in the interior of Brazil, in the district north of Pernambuco and south of the Amazon. It is the carrier of the dreaded "jungle" fever. The Institute of Tropical Diseases in Rio is working to eliminate this fever; so is the Rockefeller Institute, but many people are dying of it. If it is not checked, it may spread to Panama and to our own southern states.

*   *   *   *   *

The next day we visit Santos, Brazil's big coffee port. It is on the coast, two thousand feet below São Paulo, and to get there we ride on one of the most remarkable railroads in the world. No other railroad has such a steep grade. Part of the way we go by cable car. From the windows of the car we look straight down into the jungle, look down on it from a great height. Seeing the tall trees, the tangled undergrowth, the trailing lianas, we realize what a tremendous task it was to clear the way for this railroad, to take the rails along the sides of hills and on trestle bridges over deep gorges. It is so lovely to look into the treetops! The slopes beneath us and the *serra* on the other side of the valley are thickly dotted with flowering trees: yellow acacia, the purple Lenten trees

that are now in flower all over Brazil, pink trees, white trees.
The whole forest seems a garden. A light rain falls and the
pleasant smell of damp earth and dripping foliage comes to
us through the window of the train.

As we go down into the valley it grows warmer. We find
ourselves going through vast banana plantations. Close to the
train tracks grow the trees with their broad green leaves, each
tree bearing one large bunch of bananas. When the bunch
is cut, the tree also is cut down, a new tree springs from the
root. A narrow river winds among the trees, boats come along
it laden with bunches of green bananas. Bananas are always
picked when they are still green, partly to save them from the
birds, partly because ripe bananas could not easily be shipped
successfully.

Santos is a contrast to big, modern São Paulo, for it is not
a large city and the streets are narrow and quaint. At the
wharves, bags and bags of coffee are being loaded on boats.

"But this is nothing," they tell us. "The war has made
things very different. The port of Santos is no longer busy."
We see that this is true, for there are not many ships, and the
houses are in need of paint. The whole city seems like a city
asleep—a city waiting for something that does not come.

Santos is not only a coffee port; it has fine bathing beaches
and the Paulistas come down here for sea bathing. The beaches
go on for miles. We drive for quite a distance along the sand.

There is an orchid garden with hundreds of different vari-
eties of orchids, and, though this is not the flowering season, a
few of the loveliest ones are in bloom. Against a dark tree trunk
gleams the pure white flower of one of the rarest orchids in the
world.

DOWN TO RIO

A T São Paulo airport, when we are waiting for the plane
to Rio, we meet our first young Cariocas. Carioca was
the name that the Indians gave to a part of early Rio,
it means "house of the white man." Now all the people of Rio call themselves Cariocas.

Our young Cariocas are two and six years old. They have
been to São Paulo to visit their grandparents and they are returning with their mother to Rio. A crowd of relatives sees
them off. The children pay little attention to the family because they are so attracted by the bright blue-and-yellow
macaws that sidle up and down the veranda rail of the airport.

"A-ra-ra!" the birds say hoarsely, and *arara* is their Brazilian name. Brazil is full of bright birds; all kinds of parrots,
big-billed toucans, gay little hummingbirds. But the *araras*,
with their absurdly decorated faces, are great favorites. A cage
full of them in brilliant blues and greens and yellows is there
to welcome arrivals at the Rio airport.

The plane comes. Our little Cariocas kiss all the relatives;
the boy bends over, with a pretty gesture, and kisses his grand-

father's hand. We go aboard. Small Maria Elisa has a seat
to herself; her short legs stick out straight, but she sits there
with great dignity and even has her own box lunch.

It is a dreamlike flight down to Rio, a short flight of a little
over an hour.

"There is Rio harbor!" We can't help being thrilled over
that. The plane circles the harbor to lose altitude. There is
the Sugar Loaf! We recognize the strange, bare rock from the
many pictures we have seen of it. There is *Corcovado*, "the
Hunchback," on the summit of which stands a magnificent
statue of Christ, with arms out-
stretched in blessing.

We glide down and land at the
Airport Santos Dumont. This airport is one of the finest in the world.
Most cities say, "There isn't space
for an airport in the city; we must
build it outside." But Rio thought
differently. A hill that did not seem
at all useful in the center of the
town was levelled and the earth
from it used to form a peninsula
jutting out into the bay. This makes
a central landing place for both sea
and land planes, and Rio has worked
hard to make this airport a fitting
introduction to the city. Not only are
the buildings handsome, but there
are also pergolas leading to the sea-

plane docks; arbors, palms, and flowering trees. Even the sidewalks outside the buildings make a lovely pattern, their concrete square criss-crossed by ribbons of green grass. There is
an air-conditioned restaurant which is a favorite luncheon place
for Cariocas on steamy summer days.

As we make our landing, we can see the crowd waiting at the
airport. Our Carioca family, which has been so quiet, suddenly begins to chatter and almost bursts with excitement.

"See!" says the mother, hurrying Maria's small hands into
tiny white gloves. "There is Papai! He sees us! Wave to
him!" When they land, what a reunion there is! South American families are not at all ashamed to show their affection for
each other; in Brazil one notices it more, because, of all Latin-
American peoples, Brazilians are the most demonstrative.

Many books we have read state that Brazil is the friendliest
of the South American countries. Brazilians express themselves
more freely, and they are undoubtedly very friendly and cor-
dial, but we have found a friendly welcome everywhere. No-
where could we find kinder and more thoughtful people than
in Peru. So it is best not to make comparisons.

It is very hot in Rio, and we are glad that we are staying at
a waterfront hotel with a large balcony outside our room. From
the balcony we look out over the harbor with its many islands.
We see the airport and the planes constantly circling the bay.
Over there are the lovely Organ Mountains. One peak, reaching up towards the sky, looks like the index finger of a hand—
it is "the Finger of God." Almost all the time clouds gather
stormily over the mountains and there are sudden, heavy rain-
storms. Cariocas call this "the month of rains." "Only after

we have had plenty of rain will cool weather come," they tell us.

Below our balcony, curving around the bay, is the wide sweep of Rio's waterfront drive, Avenida Beira Mar. Buses and taxis tear along it at great speed. Crossing it with some difficulty, we take a bus that soon turns inland and goes along Avenida Rio Branco, the wide street with its double row of trees that runs through the heart of Rio. As we step from the bus, here are the famuos mosaic sidewalks, adapted from those of Portugal, made of black and white stones carefully fitted into patterns. The sidewalks fascinate us so that we almost bump into the passersby. The favorite pattern is the one like waves of the sea, so often photographed, but there are also flowers and butterflies and many other designs.

There are public buildings on the Avenida. One of them is the big National Library, considered the finest library in South America.

Most of the shops are on the narrow side streets, and in some of these streets wheeled traffic is prohibited. There are many jewelers' shops with rings and pins and necklaces made from Brazilian stones. Brazil is rich in semi-precious stones, especially amethyst, topaz, and the lovely bright blue Brazilian aquamarine. There are precious stones too. The third largest diamond in the world was found in Brazil and named the *Vargas* diamond after Brazil's president. This diamond was said to resemble the map of Brazil in shape, and it is at present in the United States being cut into smaller stones and polished.

At the end of this narrow street a surprise awaits us, for here is the flower market. It is a big building with individual stalls or small shops full of flowers. The great feature of the market, however, is the funeral wreaths. Although they cost only about two dollars in our money, these wreaths are enormous. They are six or eight feet tall and wide. Many of them are made of fern and palm leaves, silvered; others add flowers. We have seen several funerals and noticed that it is necessary to have a *truck* to carry the wreaths. We watch two Carioca women buying huge bouquets of flowers which would fill the whole window of one of our florist shops. The flowers are wrapped carefully in cellophane and carried home by a delivery man. The women stick a few carnations—a goodwill gift from the owner of the stall—in their hair and trot home behind the enormous bouquets.

Flowers grow luxuriantly in Rio, almost every house has its garden, and we wonder why people ever have to buy them. Possibly these people live in the tall, very modern apartment houses that we see in some parts of the city.

It is too hot to stay in the city very long, so we go to the Botanical Gardens where we think it will be cool. There are the magnificent avenues of tall royal palms with mountains behind them and the Christ on Corcovado looking down. These palms grew from the seed of one palm brought to Rio by the Portuguese emperor Dom João V. The mother palm is still alive and great care is taken of her. Now her many children make the principal cities of Brazil beautiful. Rio has several avenues of these palms and one of them leads to the President's palace. A picture of President Vargas is pasted on the trunk of each tree; we do not know why, except that one sees pictures of him everywhere. In no other South American country is one so conscious of the personality of the President. He has absolute power, but, say the Brazilians, why should one worry about that? He makes good laws and is a good president.

Certainly Brazil is a progressive country. No opportunity for civic development seems to be wasted. Even as we sit in the Botanical Gardens in the shade of beautiful trees, we notice that the benches give us advice. Painted on the back of one is the legend:

"In planting a tree you serve your country."

and on another:

"Sow the seeds of civilization and then take care of them."

Our first night in Rio is one of wonder and beauty, for on this night the moon is full. We sit on our balcony watching it rise over Guanabara Bay and hang like a golden lantern in the sky. A necklace of lights shines along the curving shore drive; the lights from the skyscrapers are reflected in the water. We could do without the neon signs that go on and off, also without the impudent little boat that goes up and down the bay, its changing neon signs advertising maté tea. "Maté" says the sign one minute. Then on comes the picture of a lion. The connection is not quite clear. Will one become as strong as a lion on South American tea? We try some of it, iced. It does taste something like tea, only more smoky. We decide that it would take time to acquire a taste for it.

We experiment with other Brazilian foods. The coffee, as at São Paulo, is strange to us. It is black and strong, served in tiny doll-sized cups. To make it drinkable, one must put in much sugar. Then there are many different vegetables. *Palmito*, the one we like best, is hearts of palm, served as a salad. The fruits

are even more interesting than the vegetables. For every meal
one may have oranges, peeled whole; melons, papaya, mangoes
—if one cares to chance eating this juicy yellow fruit in public—
bananas, big and little. There is *cajú*, a preserve made of the
pear-shaped fruit of the cajú tree, known elsewhere as cashew.
And there is a terribly sweet mixture of orange and shredded
coconut that always appears on the menu; it is what we call
"ambrosia" but much sweeter.

*   *   *   *   *

For the rest of our stay in Rio we have as our informal guide
Senhorita R., a young Carioca whom we met in the States.
Nothing is too much trouble for her; she is delighted to show
us the city of which she is so proud.

One morning we ride out to see the famous Copacabana
Beach. It *is* a beautiful place and here we see, instead of a
boardwalk, long stretches of black-and-white mosaic sidewalk
following the line of the beach.

Another morning, Senhorita R. arrives without a hat.

"We are going to the *feira livre*," she says. "We don't wear
hats to the *feira*, that would look too dressed up."

The *feira livre*, or free market, is held in towns all over
Brazil. It is a movable street market. The vendors are licensed
and are allowed to set up the market in certain streets on certain
days. The one we go to is on the waterfront in the Flamengo
section of Rio. Under the trees in the public square, against the
near background of the sea, and the distant background of the
Sugar Loaf, many little booths are set up. Each booth has a
blue-and-white-striped awning. Each vendor wears the white
cap and apron required by the Board of Health.

Here is a stall full of dresses and hats. At this one there are crates of live chickens. Another sells nothing but long bars of soap for washing clothes, another dried meat, another noodles. The miniature "grocery stores," with their brooms and colored dustclothes, household articles and canned goods are the gayest of all.

An old woman stops to buy a broom. "Thank you," she says to the vendor. "And God go with you."

Mistresses and maids come to the *feira* for a week's supply of fruit and vegetables. They walk away carrying their purchases in the brightly decorated burlap bags provided by each stall for a few cents. Some hire the "carriers," boys with huge baskets carried on the head, to take their purchases home.

"My mother doesn't send her maid to the market alone," says Senhorita R. "She has too many boy-friends here and would stay too long, talking!" We are sitting on a bench, while the

artist sketches. Suddenly she comes back to us in great agitation.

"You've got to come with me," she says to Senhorita R. "They don't like me to draw them. They come around and say things, and they glare at me." Senhorita R. laughs, but she goes back to the market with the artist and soon discovers what is the trouble. To begin with, if one has sugar-cane or palmito or melons to *sell*, it is a bit bewildering to have a stranger stand by one's stall and *draw* these things. Then the artist had not only been sketching, she had been writing color notes on her pad. The vendors thought she was a government inspector, for, having dark eyes and hair, she passed for a Brazilian.

A few explanatory words from Senhorita R. and the vendors are friendly once more. This is the first time the artist has had any difficulty. Usually the country people gather around and look on, or follow at her heels, smiling delightedly and saying, "Look just like real," or "How fast she draws!"

At noon there is feverish activity, for the *feira livre* must close. Awnings are rolled up, stalls taken down, everything is loaded on trucks. In an hour's time the square shows no sign at all of the busy market.

On the streets of Rio one sees "walking shops" too. The

broom man is laden with brooms and wastebaskets. The artificial flower man carries artificial flowers and paper lamp shades.
Vendors of fruit and vegetables carry two large baskets on a
yoke over their shoulders.

Then there is also the big market, by the docks, where everything under the sun seems to be sold and where brightly painted
fishing boats are constantly unloading fresh fish and the shrimps
that are so popular with Cariocas.

It would not occur to us to take a Sunday excursion across the
bay, but Senhorita R. says that to go to Paquetá on the Sunday
ferry is the way to see the people—and it is.

Paquetá is a lovely little island, one of the hundred or more
in Guanabara Bay. Some people live there all the year round,
but it is mostly a summer resort. For the working classes of Rio
it is a pleasant Sunday excursion. The ferryboat takes an hour
and a half each way, but the round-trip fare is only a few cents.

We go on the ferry with a large, assorted crowd. Some are
Portuguese, some Negro, many
are mestiço (mixed). All are
friendly, all are together and
we realize that there is no "color
line" in Brazil.

The crowd is gay and cheerful. A boy plays the guitar and
sings carnival songs. A man
comes by selling bright-colored
balls. He has large, feathered
shuttlecocks used for the game
known as *peteca* pinned up and

down his coat. *Peteca* is a favorite game played by batting the shuttlecock back and forth with the hand. A boy and girl come by with their little brother; they buy him a ball. The boy is in the white dress uniform of one of the high schools; he looks like a young naval officer.

There are many boys and girls of high-school age. The girls have every style of hair-do; the artist sketches them surreptitiously. At the island, the crowd scatters, going to the many beaches. We drive around the island in an old-fashioned carriage and have lunch at a blue-painted waterfront restaurant—an "all-Brazilian" lunch with fresh coconut milk, shrimps and rice and *goiabada* (guava paste). From our table we can watch the holiday-makers dancing the *samba* on the beach to the music of a guitar.

We leave early to avoid the homeward-bound crowd. As we go back across the beautiful bay, young men sit on the rail of the ferryboat and sing a haunting carnival song: "Brasil—Brasil———"

On the last evening that we are in Rio we go up the Sugar Loaf. First we drive with Senhorita R. to the Urca district to visit her small cousins. The houses in this district cluster around the tall, rocky Urca hill. We stop at a small white house, pass through the green arched gateway of its hedge, and find twelve-year-old Maria waiting for us on the porch. She has put on her carnival costume for us to see; it is the colorful costume of the Negroes of Bahia, in northern Brazil. Maria looks very charming in it, her big brown eyes

are bright with excitement, her lips are red, her cheeks pink.

"She doesn't wear make-up except with the carnival costume," her mother explains.

We would like to make a longer visit, but we must leave if we want to get to Sugar Loaf in time for the illumination. At the Urca station of the aerial railroad we get into the small, almost square car that is to swing us through space, first to the top of the Urca and then to the top of Sugar Loaf.

As the car swings out into space on a double cable, it sways, for the wind is quite high. The motorman tells us that there is no danger, in a very high wind the car does not run, but this wind is not strong enough to damage the cable. We hope not! This swinging through space is almost as exciting as the airplane, in fact it is more startling to look down. As we reach the top of the Urca it seems as if the car would go right into the bare, grim rock, but instead it swings gently into a station cut in the side of the hill. We take another car, swing into space once more and find ourselves at the summit of the Sugar Loaf.

We stand on the observation platform and look down over Rio and over Guanabara Bay. It is half-past six and we are waiting for "the illumination." Suddenly it begins. A necklace of lights is flung around the shoreline of Rio, district by district. The curve of Gloria is lighted, then Flamengo and Copacabana. Across the bay the lights come on. In the interior they twinkle like fireflies. Last of all, at seven o'clock the Christ on Corcovado is floodlighted. There has been nothing at all to be seen on the black mountain, then, in a moment, the tall statue shines white against the dark sky, arms outstretched in quiet blessing over the glittering city. We have been saying all the usual, commonplace things—"How lovely," "How beautiful," but now there is nothing we can say, so we are quite silent.

It is all so lovely that we hate to leave it, but we must go down. On the way, Senhorita R. tells us about the little girl who lives in Rio and is called *Senhorita Pao d'Assucar*, Miss Sugar Loaf. Her father was a silhouette artist who cut pictures of tourists who came to Sugar Loaf, and Paulina—that is her real name—was born in a house at the top of the rock and lived there until she was two years old.

"Are you glad you have been up Sugar Loaf?" Senhorita R. asks us. "Glad?" we say, "don't let any one miss it. Every one who comes to Rio *must* see the illumination."

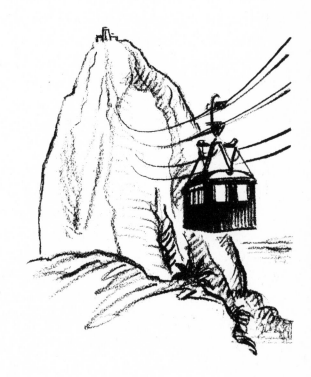

Up THE COAST OF BRAZIL

BAHIA, CITY OF CHURCHES

BAHIA is the old capital of Brazil; Bahia is a bit of old Portugal; Bahia is strange and different—and we are on our way there! Like many of the towns on the Brazilian coast, Bahia has two names, a "dress up" name, and an everyday name which is not really the name of the town but of the state. Bahia's full name is really *São Salvador da Bahia de Todos os Santos*, Holy Savior of all Saints' Bay.

This time our plane is a "Baby Clipper," a small twelve-passenger seaplane used for local stops all along the coast from Rio to Pará. We could fly across country in a Douglas and save time, but we want to see the coast.

When we start, we notice that the day is cloudy and somewhat foggy, but we do not think much about it. After flying for two hours, the plane begins to glide down for a landing.

"This must be Victoria," we say. "What a beautiful harbor, just like Rio. Why, the airport is like the one at Rio!"

Then our astonished eyes read the sign:

AIRPORT SANTOS DUMONT

We *are* in Rio! Certainly, for there is the market.

We ask puzzled questions. "Yes, we had to come back," the purser tells us. "We had word by radio that there was too much fog for us to land at Victoria. You will wait here at the airport until we can start again."

Until now the weather has been so good that we have not learned how careful Pan-American is of its passengers and planes. Pilots do not take off in stormy weather; they do not land in fog or fly after dark. To make a "blind" landing on the harbor at Victoria, full of small native craft, would be dangerous.

We wait an hour, then go aboard once more, three hours late on our trip north. This time we make our landing at Victoria with the sun shining brightly. And the airport is *not* like Rio!

Our next stop is at Caravellos, but we fly for quite a while before reaching it. Along the coast there are thousands of coconut palms, behind them savannahs and forests alternate. Behind the coastal plain is the fertile land where cacao grows. Rivers wind through the country looking like brown or yellow snakes, according to the color of the mud they carry. Where they enter the sea, its pale green water is colored by the mud for a long way out. Each river brings down so much mud that it has a delta at its mouth. The desert coast of Peru, the green coast of Brazil—where could one find greater contrast?

Caravellos is a strange little town, with a small white shack for an airport. It is *hot*. On the muddy beach very long dug-outs are drawn up. Crabs scuttle about in the ooze. In contrast to all this is our one passenger from Caravellos. João is about ten years old and travelling alone to the naval school in Bahia. His cadet's uniform is sky-blue and white, very smart, even to spats and white gloves! He seems perfectly self-possessed and chats with the purser most of the way. At Bahia he is met by friends and goes off in a sky-blue taxi that matches his uniform.

We thought that we knew all there was to know about the ways of South American taxi drivers, but Bahia adds a new hazard. Here the drivers not only drive *fast*, but drive *on* the trolley tracks, two wheels on each track. This calls for skill; it works fairly well until a trolley, also going at a good speed, comes unexpectedly around the corner.

Bahia is all that we expect it to be and more. The pink and yellow and blue and green houses of other towns have here added statues along their roofs or around their walls so that they look for all the world like frosted cakes. The fronts of other houses are of blue and white Portuguese tile. Even the gate-posts have statues of dogs, or stone pineapples. In fact, Bahia holds the record for statutes; they are everywhere and on everything.

There are really two cities of Bahia, the lower one by the docks, the upper, residential one at the top of the hill. The two are connected by a huge concrete shaft in which is an *elevador* that takes one in a few seconds and for a few cents from one level to another. People go by elevator, but cars and wagons wind their long, steep way up the narrow streets that lead from one level to another. Even in the upper town the streets are so incredibly narrow and steep that, standing at the top of some of them, it seems as if it would be impossible to make the descent without wings. Everywhere, uphill and down, ramble black-and-white mosaic sidewalks such as we first saw in Rio.

Quito is old Spain, Bahia is old Portugal with a very great deal of Africa. The Negroes, who make up the larger part of the population, are the descendants of the Negro slaves brought here when the city was the center of Brazil's slave trade. They are still very black and very African. The women wear a distinctive costume, a bright-colored skirt with a loose sack blouse, often white and trimmed with lace. A scarf or shawl is slung over one shoulder or tied around the waist. On festival days the costume is more elaborate, bracelets, bead necklaces, and earrings being added to it. The men wear bright-colored or striped jerseys.

The most thrilling place in all Bahia is the waterfront. To look down on the harbor from the upper town is like looking at the stage-set for a puppet show. There is the sea wall, the round toylike fort, the wharf with tall-masted boats moored against it. The bay is full of sailboats, big ones, little ones, many of them with triangular sails. Even the naval training school, by the wharf, looks like a yellow toy castle. In front

of it drill the cadets in their bright blue uniforms, and from this height they, too, look like toys. We feel that when the show is over we shall want to reach over and pack fort and castle, ships and soldiers neatly away in their box.

When we take the elevator down to the lower level, the toylike aspect has gone. Here is a waterfront that teems with life, that sparkles with color. From under a shady tree we look down at the boats and see everything that is going on. We watch them for hours. As the artist sketches she is conscious that a black cloud seems to have gathered around her, but every one is friendly and good-natured.

The boats are painted in bright or once-bright colors. A few of the names show imagination: *Song of the Bird*, *Star of Peace*, *God Who Guides Us*. Some of the boats have brought in loads of wood, some are piled high with sugar cane and bananas. A tiny marmoset peers impishly at us from a basket to which he is chained. Each boat has its simple cooking apparatus, a small iron charcoal-burning stove.

From the wharf men are throwing terra cotta earthenware jars to other men on a boat. Not a jar is dropped or broken. The boat is piled high with jars of all sizes, the big ones ornamented with handsome designs. We wonder where they are going. A day or two later we find them at the water's edge in another part of town. Here is a *feira livre* with thousands of jars, bowls, and dishes piled high. Who will buy them all? There are few tourists in Bahia. But the jars cost only a few cents and Bahianas themselves buy them. The people use the

133

jars and dishes for water, for cooking, for every purpose. We
see little girls playing tea-party with some of the tiny dishes.

The life of the waterfront changes constantly. A man goes
by with a performing monkey. It is a very black monkey with
a pink dress and a straw hat. Other men sell parrots of all sizes
and colors. "*Louro! louro!*" the parrots say instead of "Polly."
"*Papagaio louro*" means "yellow parrot." The birds usually
drop the "*papagaio*" and call themselves "yellow."

Patient, gray donkeys come by with panniers full of juicy
oranges. We notice that the oranges here are seedless; it was
from Bahian oranges that our California ones were developed.

When—if ever—we are tired of watching the boats and people, we go into the big market building. In here are all kinds
of foods and all kinds of smells. Some stalls sell only the
wooden clogs that make a pleasant clatter on Bahian cobbled
streets. We buy dolls in native costume and several of the
carved hands that Bahianas wear "to keep off the evil eye."
The Negroes here keep many of their African customs and
superstitions. In villages outside the town, strange African
dances still take place, and there are still mysterious religious
cults.

But Bahia is also modern in many ways. We visit the very
up-to-date Cocoa Institute. "Yes," the man who shows us
over it tells us, "Bahia is second in the world in production of
cocoa. Yes, the war has hurt trade, but the United States is
one of our largest customers. The United States uses chocolate
for so many things." Possibly the first chocolate soda that we
have on our return will be made of cocoa beans from Bahia!

The Normal School of the State of Bahia is completely
modern, its new buildings outdoing in modern architecture any-

thing we have seen in school buildings of our own country. In the demonstration school, the children wear the school uniforms of all Brazil, white blouses and dark blue pleated skirts for girls, white shirts and blue trousers for boys. In the open-air kindergarten the children wear white aprons with their names embroidered in red. The children vary from cream-colored to inky black; the teachers are both Portuguese and colored. Petromio, a small cream-colored boy, beams at us. Dagmar Barbara is a little Negro girl with stiff pigtails. Regina is as blonde as she can be, with yellow hair and blue eyes.

To leave the modern and go back to the past, we visit some of Bahia's churches. Brazilians will tell you that there are three hundred and sixty-five churches in Bahia, but there are really only about eighty. Eighty churches is a good many; there is a church at the end of every street and around every corner, and they are not like other churches in any other part of South America.

We go into the sixteenth-century church of São Francisco and are so astonished that for a few minutes we can't speak. For the whole church is decorated with carved jacaranda wood in high relief, and the wood is painted in colors and in gold. Each wall, each chapel billows with angels and cherubs, and strange, women with beads around their necks. On the pulpit are fat little angels with pink and blue ballet skirts. Among the angels are exotic birds and flowers. We see something of this excessive but interesting decoration in other Bahian churches, but none of them can equal São Francisco. In strange contrast to the billowing, blossoming church is the quiet little Franciscan brother who shows us around.

It is in church that we see two young Bahianas who are the color of ebony. As we sit in a church by the waterfront watching the people come in, we notice that many of the colored people go to a chapel on one side of the church. A very black little girl comes in and kneels before the altar, putting down the very small bundle of vegetables she has bought in the market. We move nearer and see that she is praying to a tiny Virgin as black as herself. The Virgin is quite crudely made, but she wears a golden crown and a cloak of heavenly blue. She was found in the ground and that, they *say*, accounts for her color. However that may be, the Negroes undoubtedly feel that she is their own.

In the afternoon at the Chapel of Graça, one of the oldest churches, benediction is being sung. All the altar boys are Negro, the one who lights the candles is as dark as the robe beneath his surplice. He lights the candles with care, and then he carries them to the altar, pride in every step.

We stop a moment in the vestry of this church to see a picture said to be the first one painted in Brazil. It is interesting to us because it tells a story similar to our story of John Smith and Pocahontas. In the background is a sinking ship, a white man who has landed from it is being attacked by Indians and rescued by an Indian princess in a feathered headdress and skirt. Diogo Alves Correira *was*, it seems, rescued by an

Indian chief's daughter and afterwards married her. The story goes on to tell that the princess, baptized Catherina, dreamed that a beautiful Virgin would be found in the sunken ship. It was to this Virgin that our little ebony altar boy was lighting candles.

Two of the most interesting churches in Bahia are at the edge of the city; both are churches of the sea. Nosso Senhor do Bonfim, Our Lord of the Good Ending, is where sailors came to give thanks for a successful voyage. Each year the Negroes, in their gayest clothes, go to Bonfim to scrub the church and prepare it for its annual festival.

In one small chapel at Bonfim there are votive offerings made by those who believe they have been saved from illness or disaster. They are far cruder than those of the churches of Europe. From the ceiling hang plaster casts of legs, mostly showing the effects of snake bite. There are primitive drawings and paintings. These are so realistic that the room is quite a little chamber of horrors. Our favorite is a crude watercolor showing a tiger advancing towards a terrified Negro family who, too frightened to move, are clutching their children to their bosoms. We are full of curiosity about this. What saved the family? What fate overtook the tigers?

As we go out of the church we notice that the women cover their heads with bits of black or white netting, sometimes bound around the edges with colored ribbon. Possibly this is a survival of the old way in which the servants of a household decorated their

head coverings. In Spanish countries the mistress wore the
mantilla, the maids wore a simpler head covering. To make
this more attractive, the material was embroidered or bound
around the edge with ribbon. This may also apply to Portuguese countries. A soft breeze blows into the church and the
door frames a picture of blue sea and tall palm trees. The voices
of the choir boys are piercingly sweet. A pleasant place, Bonfim. It must have seemed a pleasant haven after a long voyage.

We go on to the charming unspoiled little chapel of Nossa
Senhora do Montserrate, so close to the water's edge that waves
wash over the walls of its churchyard. It is growing dusk, now,
and the tiny lighthouse on the churchyard wall twinkles out
across the bay. Above the chapel is the old fort of Montserrate.
It is even more toylike than the fort in Bahia harbor; at any
moment we expect to see four tin sentries march stiffly from the
four sentry boxes.

ADVENTURE ON THE COAST

FLYING up the coast from Bahia to Pará, we have what *we* consider an adventure.

Fog delays the plane that is to take us to Pernambuco, the real name of which is Recife in the state of Pernambuco. "We can't make Recife tonight," the purser says. "We'll fly as long as we have daylight, then set you down somewhere along the coast."

Travelling men sit and tell gloomy stories of places at which they have been "set down." At six o'clock, just as the sun sets, we come down at a floating dock in the mouth of a river. On one side of the bay is a town with a long row of pastel-colored houses and a long row of trees cut into neat oblong shapes. On the other side of the river the shore is fringed with coconut palms, and bonfires burn between thatched, native huts. It doesn't seem real.

"What town is this?" we ask the purser.

"Aracajú."

"Has it a hotel?"

"Oh, a sort of *pension*, I believe. Don't know what it's like because I've never been here."

We go ashore in a boat. Crowds are at the landing stage to meet us. We walk in procession to the hotel; the two of us, two travelling salesmen; a Venezuelan family consisting of grandmother, father, mother, three aunts, and José, aged fourteen months. The populace of Aracajú walks with us.

The "hotel" is clean and better than we expected. In the dining room, the main decoration is a huge electric refrigerator on which is a magnificent vase of flowers. It produces bottles of beer and the worst mineral water we have ever tasted. Ordinary water is, of course, more of a risk than we care to take in this part of the country.

"Put a spoon of sugar in it," advises one of the salesmen. "It will take out the gas. We travel up the Amazon and, when the water isn't drinkable, you have to learn all the tricks." We put in the sugar. The *gas* bubbles out, but the *taste* stays.

The local band plays outside the hotel until midnight, the beds are like rock; mosquitoes keep us awake until about one o'clock. At three, there is a loud knocking at all our doors, and the hotel proprietor warns us it is time to get up. But his clock is an hour wrong, and when we come, sleepy-eyed, from our rooms we find that the plane does not leave until five. The moon is still shining on the water. Only José is calm about it; he is asleep in his father's arms. We sit and wait; then, at half-past four, still in semi-darkness, we go off to the float. "Breakfast" is a tiny cup of coffee served on the float by the light of

140

the purser's flashlight. Two hours later, at Pernambuco, we find a table set with coffee, toast, cake, huge glasses of orange juice, cheese, and, to our delight, HAM AND EGGS! Pernambuco was once Dutch, and this probably accounts for the cheese at breakfast. With its many canals and waterways, the town reminds us a little of one in Holland.

The day that follows is never to be forgotten. We fly for thirteen hours, in the small, stuffy plane, coming down many times to deliver mail. Sometimes there is a float, sometimes a boat comes off to meet us. The air is rough, and every one except José is airsick. "I've never been sick," says the purser bitterly. "But if this sort of thing keeps up, I shall be."

Soon every member of José's family is in a state of collapse. He stands in the middle of the wreckage, kisses his mother's hand, says pitifully, "Mamita! Papito!" They pull themselves together and try their best to be nice to the baby. We have a picture of the typically devoted South American family, for they never lose patience with him or with each other. José is patient, too, and it is not until the thirteenth hour that he gives way to a tantrum that is one of the best we have seen. By this time, he hates his whole family. His dark eyes flash. From grandmother to the youngest aunt, he beats them with his little fists. He hates the world. We all feel much the way he does and envy him because he can take it out in screams and kicks.

Although we are tired, we cannot help being fascinated by the Amazonian jungle over which we are now flying. We thought we had seen jungle before, but this is

the real thing. We are flying low enough to see the tremendous trees that reach their branches above other tall trees growing so closely together that they look like a thickly woven mat.

And then at last we are at Pará, or Belém, to use its right name. Santa Maria de Belém—never was there a stranger setting for a Bethlehem, here at the mouth of the Amazon, at the edge of the jungle. This is the port of the rubber-growing region. A little over a hundred years ago the first few pairs of rubber shoes were made by the Indians of Pará and shipped to the United States. When the rubber trade was at its height, Belém was a rich and proud city. When rubber was grown in other parts of the world, the city's great prosperity was over. Even now it is a dignified and a beautiful city. The jungle seems to be here with us, for the streets are double-lined with mango trees, old mango trees, mildewed by the constant rain, dripping with moisture, dripping with parasites. Green mangoes hang from the trees; we wonder what happens when they ripen, for there isn't anything so slippery underfoot as a good, ripe, juicy mango. Perhaps the appetites of little Negro boys take care of that.

Reaching the hotel, we are quite revived by the sight of beds with inner-spring mattresses, and after a night's sleep we are fresh and cheerful again. The morning is rainy and we look down from our window on dozens of umbrellas bobbing along. There must be a girls' school near by, for under the umbrellas are dozens of girls in blue-and-white uniforms. They seem quite unconcerned about the rain; they probably walk to school in it many days of the year.

Drip, drip, drip! The leaves of the mango trees shine in

the rain, their old trunks are wet and dark. There is something indescribable about the wetness of a mango tree. More than ever it seems as if the jungle were marching up to our very door. We wonder if the city were deserted how long it would take the jungle to march completely over it and swallow it up.

The road to the airport is through the jungle. A scientist has said that it is difficult to see the jungle, for one cannot really see it from the air, and when one is in it the trailing vines and the parasites almost hide the trees. For a jungle is not merely a forest, there is the thick undergrowth and there are the tree ferns and the strange plants that grow up the trees and on them, and the vines that grow from tree to tree. Driving through it is probably as near as we shall come to being in it. We do have a very good idea of how difficult it would be to clear a path.

Leaving the city of Pará we notice, in a jungle park, a children's merry-go-round. There it stands, under the shade of the huge trees, red and yellow horses prancing under a roof of coconut thatch. Where else would we see such a thing? We carry it with us as our last clear memory of South America.

THE HOMEWARD WAY

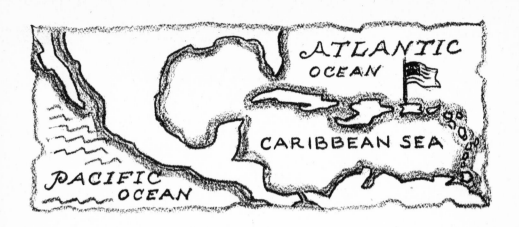

ISLANDS ON GUARD

A T THE AIRPORT, the stratoliner *Flying Cloud* is waiting for us. José and his family are there, too; they must fly through Trinidad on their way to Venezuela. However, there is plenty of room to move about on the stratoliner; it is steady, so no one is sick. José plays happily with his toy monkey and all is well.

As we take off, we are conscious of the great power of this huge plane with its four engines. We get a brief glimpse of the Amazon, it is almost hidden by fog, and except for the delta, might be the ocean.

Fog closes in and we climb rapidly to the sunlight. The stratoliner is everything that one could wish for in comfort. There are large, roomy compartments as well as single seats all along one side. The air in the plane is super-charged with air, so that, as we rise to 15,000 or 16,000 feet, we have little of that unpleasant feeling of pressure in our ears, no difficulty at all in breathing, though at first we do feel sleepy. This super-charging equalizes the pressure within the plane,

147

keeping the atmosphere as it would be if the plane were flying at 8,000 feet. When the plane comes down, the amount of outside air is gradually reduced and the air kept cool, so that the descent is as comfortable as it can be made.

Everything on the *Flying Cloud* is de luxe, and we have every kind of service. Lunch, skillfully served, is the best we have had aloft. And we fly at such a speed! As there are no clouds we do not need to go any higher than 15,000 feet. It seems no time at all until we see the mountains of Trinidad—those mountains that Columbus was so glad to see after a long and weary third voyage.

Now I am almost as excited as I was on the day we crossed the Andes, for Trinidad is my childhood home. I think of a poem that I wrote when I was nine. It was called "The Discovery of Trinidad" and I smile when I think how fine it sounded to me then. It ended, I remember, in a grand flourish of words:

> Trinidad that island, a wonderful gift from on high;   2
> Was a token of how Heaven answered a man's despairing cry;
> And she has ever prospered and ever won renown,
> For the island of Columbus is the flower of England's crown.

"Where," said my father, looking at me suspiciously as he read it, "*where* did you get that 'flower of England's crown'?" "Out of the guide book," I admitted.

If Trinidad is not "the fairest flower," it is at least one of the most beautiful of the West Indian Islands. It is, of course, a piece of the South American continent that became separated from the mainland through some volcanic disturbance. In Trinidad's forests are the same tall *ceiba* (silk-cotton) trees that one sees in Brazil, the same birds fly among them, the same snakes slide through the undergrowth, the same flowers grow everywhere. The names of the towns, Port-of-Spain, San Fernando, San Juan, tell of the time when the island was part of Spanish America.

The Pan-American airport is quite a long way from the capital city, Port-of-Spain. It is new and unfinished. Next to it is a training station for British pilots and we realize with a sudden shock that here is a country at war. Not only the customs inspector comes to look at our baggage, but the censor comes to examine our papers. Fortunately he knows who I am. "John Dalgliesh's daughter? Oh, that's all right, I don't have to go through *your* things." We sigh with relief.

At the docks in Port-of-Spain we see the tents of the American marines who have just arrived. Many Americans are arriving to work on the naval, air, and army bases that we have leased from Britain, and Trinidad is full of activity. This island, only twenty miles off the coast of Venezuela, will be one of the most important of our defenses, for it guards the southern entrance to the Panama Canal. In itself it is valuable, for it produces large quantities of oil, asphalt, sugar, cocoa.

While we are here we see a great deal of the beautiful island. For one of us it is all new, the other is interested in the changes that twenty years have brought.

When I lived here the houses were all of much the same type, not unlike those one sees in the suburbs of New Orleans. The smaller ones were always trimmed with a great deal of wooden scroll work. There are still many of these, the artist calls them "lace doily houses" and puts them in her sketchbook. But now there are also many houses in the modern style, and one modern apartment house.

Even the hotel, once rambling and tropical looking, has been modernized and is quite American. Our room is on an enclosed garden court and, after many rooms that were on noisy main streets, it seems a haven of restfulness.

"How quiet it is!" we say thankfully. But at six o'clock the next morning, tropical birds gather in the courtyard, with such a variety of sound we have seldom heard. "Squ-a-ak!" a piercing sound from a big black one. "Qu'est-ce qu'il dit? Qu'est-ce qu'il dit?" asks another, over and over.

Then there is the most astonishing banging of cans. What can it be? We go to the window and see that there is a cage of monkeys in the courtyard. They evidently want their breakfast and they are throwing their food cans across the cage.

There isn't any chance for more sleep, besides we have to make an early start, for we are going to drive to San Fernando, the town where I was born. So we get up and have our breakfast. After breakfast we leave, in a hired car, for our drive to the south of the island.

Our way is through many East Indian villages—hundreds of East Indians were brought here to work on the sugar estates. These people have kept their own dress, their own customs, to some extent, their own religion. "Calcutta Street" says a sign, and it *is* Calcutta Street. Outside the thatched adobe huts sit whole families of East Indians, the men in white loin cloths, the women in white or colored saris, with bracelets on arms and ankles, and gold nose rings. In the shade of trees near the huts, large zebu cattle lie peacefully. These, too, were imported from India, and so were the water buffalo that, with the cattle, do most of the work on the sugar estates.

It is crop time; the sugar cane is being cut. Large carts drawn by cattle and water buffalo are taking loads to the sugar factories. In the air, there is a pleasant smell of molasses—and the not-so-pleasant smell of cane refuse.

In one village we come upon a lovely little Hindu temple, white with bright, Indian wall paintings. Morning prayer is about to begin. In the tiny single room of the temple is a small altar. It is all set about with flowers, and in each flower a small

candle is burning. They happen to be pink birthday candles; so the whole effect is not unlike a birthday cake.

The priest's assistant invites us to come near. "But you may not come in with shoes on your feet," he says; so we stand in the doorway. He rings a bell and blows long, weird notes on a conch shell. No one comes, but prayers are conducted whether the village people come or not. The priest, an old man with a gray beard, wears only a loin cloth and looks like Mahatma Gandhi. He comes out of the temple with a large spoon in which fat is burning. This he offers solemnly to the Hindu gods painted on the outer walls of the temple, including a peacock painted on each side of the doorway. He goes in again, and we hear him chanting a prayer. Then all is silent, we make a contribution to the temple and go on. A little farther along there is another temple, so tiny that it seems impossible for a priest to get inside it.

We drive through Point-a-Pierre where there are large oil refineries. We are not far from La Brea, where are the oil wells and the famous Pitch Lake from which comes a good share of the world's asphalt. Huge trucks loaded with slabs of asphalt pass our car. Like the banana trucks of Colombia, they almost crowd us off the road.

In San Fernando we visit the delightful old house where I used to live; it is high up on a hill overlooking the harbor. From its windows we look down on the charming town with its red roofs. There are the three red church steeples that, as a child, I tried to draw, and never could get them just right. Beyond them is the sea, and on the horizon we can see the dim outlines of the mountains of Venezuela. The house is now the

teachers' house of the Canadian East-Indian Mission School. There are fine school buildings and a most attractive group of East Indian, Negro and Chinese girls in neat school uniforms. The principal of the school asks me to talk to the older girls. They question me about the books I have written for children. It is fun to be able to tell them that my first and only "poem" was written *here*. I was standing on the gallery of the house looking across at the Andes when I made it up and thinking how silly it was that Columbus didn't know South America when he saw it!

When we leave the house we go down to the market. It is one of the most attractive mar-
kets we have seen. East Indian
women squat on the ground in
the middle of carefully ar-
ranged "islands" of vegetables.

"Why *didn't* you tell me
that you grew up in a place like
this?" asks the artist. "No wonder you felt at home in South
America! Why this is Colombia and Brazil with East Indians
a d d e d and some things sub-
tracted. And the little open-
faced shops we have been ad-
miring—*they are here in your
own home town.* We must do
a book about it!"

*   *   *   *   *

The stratoliner takes us swiftly and comfortably from Trinidad to Puerto Rico. As we fly over San Juan, the capital, we see the old walls and fortifications. Here is the second walled city of the Western Hemisphere, and flying over the ancient walls is our own Stars and Stripes. For two months we have not seen our flag except over an American consulate, and it is thrilling to see it here.

Earlier in the day, we were in an island that, while it is cosmopolitan, is also a little bit of Britain. Here in Puerto Rico we have a bit of America, but a good deal of old Spain. Again we hear Spanish spoken. San Juan, with its narrow streets and Spanish houses, is like towns we have seen in South America. The Spanish feeling is consciously kept, for many of the new buildings are in Spanish style.

The old walls are charming. Here are the round sentry towers that we saw guarding the walls of Cartagena and the fort of Montserrat. One of these is known as "the haunted sentry box." The story says that once a sentry disappeared from this tower leaving only his uniform. "The devil has taken

him," said the other soldiers. "We won't stand guard in *that* place."

In their day these walls served their purpose. When Spanish galleons were chased by pirates they sometimes sought refuge in San Juan harbor. Now the walls would be of little use against modern guns. But we see signs that Puerto Rico is to be one of our island defenses. Along the shore are long, ugly guns. Large naval and air stations are being built.

This is the island of Ponce de León; he was governor here and his statue stands in front of the old church where he was buried. The fine white palace in which the American general in charge of the island now lives was built by Ponce de León for his son.

Among the new buildings, the Custom House interests us and is the most cheerful and decorative custom house that it is possible to have. It is pink, built in Spanish style, with Spanish tiling on the front. It gives us quite a turn to see the American eagle lending himself to a tiled decoration! And there is a low, pink wall with pink sentry boxes built in the style of the old ones. It has its faults, this new building, but it shows more imagination than most modern ones.

We leave Puerto Rico in the same type of seaplane as the one in which we started our travels. We do not like

it quite so well after the luxury of the stratoliner. We are an an hour late getting to Miami because a storm delays us. The sun is setting, and there, in the golden light, is the International Airport. We step onto the soil of our own country with pride and a sense of achievement. We have really done it— we have flown around South America!

But our pride is a little punctured when a doctor sticks a thermometer in each mouth. Then he says sternly, "All passengers who have been in South America during the last week step into *that* room."

What are they going to do with us? Fumigate us? We step in, and a doctor says, without looking at us, "You may go." He does not have to say it twice; we leave with speed, though still wondering!

We have travelled fourteen thousand miles; and have seen many things and talked with many people. Now we are home again and have taken stock of our impressions, a few things stand out clearly. Above all, we have come back with a strong feeling of the importance of Pan-Americanism, as well as of the difficulties involved in it. The Americas *must* get to know each other, *must* stand together though this is not something that can be accomplished overnight. It began many years ago when Bolívar, making his famous crossing of the Andes, called his weary, cold, mountain-sick soldiers together. "The unity of the Americas," he told them, "is the hope of the universe." Even if there are dangers and difficulties ahead, the future must hold unity for the twenty-one republics. Young people growing up today should read intelligently, so that they will not, as some of the present generation still do, think that the language of Brazil is Spanish, or that Lima is the capital of Chile. When these young people travel in the Americas they will be different from the average tourist of the present, who does little to further friendly relations but a good deal to add to lack of understanding between the countries. We have, on this very trip, heard tourists from our own country criticizing loudly (and as if South Americans did not understand English) the ways of countries not exactly like their own. We have seen them fretting and fussing because some meal might be served a little more slowly than at home. A typical example of tourist thinking is that Latin Americans "shake hands too often." "They'll have to get over that," says the tourist cheerfully, "and learn our ways. They waste a lot of time." And what do we do with the time that we "save"?

Twenty-one Americas! The first thing we have to know is that we are only one of the twenty-one, that most of these countries are older than we are, that all those who live in the American republics have a right to call themselves Americans. Many of us still seem to think the name is ours alone. Then we must realize that we have still to work to win the friendship of the Latin-American countries. There are so many things for us to learn: the unfailing courtesy that is a part of the Latin nature; the slower but more gracious tempo at which everything moves in those countries; the ways of doing things that are different from ours; the many things we *do* have in common; the many ideals we share.

Pan Americanism doesn't mean dressing up for "fiestas" in wholly fanciful "South American" costumes. It doesn't even mean talking glibly about "our good neighbors," though these superficial things may help in their own way. It is something more essential, something deeper than that. Let's slow down and take time to find it.

"You North Americans hurry so!"

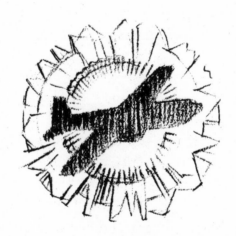